D0580334

A PORTRAIT OF AMERICAN
MOTHERS & DAUGHTERS

PHOTOGRAPHS BY RAISA FASTMAN

NewSage Press

A Portrait of American
Mothers & Daughters

Copyright ©1987
by NewSage Press

All rights reserved.
No part of this book
may be reproduced
or utilized in any form
or by any means
without permission
in writing from the
publisher.

Address inquiries to
NewSage Press
P.O. Box 41029
Pasadena, California
91104

First Edition 1987

Printed in Japan

Library of Congress
Catalog Card Number:
87-090682

ISBN 0-939165-04-X

Acknowledgements

There have been so many people who have encouraged this work over the years; I can only acknowledge a few. Foremost, I would like to thank Robin McDonnell for her years of encouragement and support, and with whose help I was able to complete this book. Audre and Herbert Mendel for sharing their friends with me, and for graciously facilitating my stay in Miami Beach. Jules Mendel, my travel agent and friend, who not only arranged my trips, but enlisted the help of her family. Mary Innes for many years of encouragement, and making sure I had a darkroom to complete this project. My editor and publisher, Maureen Michelson, for not only believing in the strength of my work, and her ceaseless encouragement, but also for her many hours of editing the written material in this book. Lucille Mendel for opening her home to me, and Loretta Ortiz y Pena for enlisting the help of her friends in New Mexico. Rachel Bat Or who helped me look into the darkness and see my own light. Susan Griffin who gave me so much encouragement in the earlier stages of this project. Pat Farbman for supporting this work without even knowing me, and Teresa Tollini for all her very special help. My deepest gratitudes to all the women who opened their hearts, their homes, and their lives to me, and allowed me to use their images.

This book is dedicated to my mother, Tema Fastman, whose relationship with me was the inspiration for this project.

Every woman is a daughter. Many women are mothers. The mother/daughter relationship is so primary, yet so little understood. Although women may be greatly influenced by their fathers, it is our mothers who are the primary role models, and no matter how differently from our mothers we may lead our lives, it is the world of women that we, as daughters, inherit. Until recently, women have not had imagery, either visual or written, that honestly reflects the experiences of daughters and mothers. In the past, the relationship was veiled in sweet sentimentality, and the conflicts and dissonance hidden from public view, and ultimately from one another. Relationships between mothers and daughters may be close or alienated, but rarely are they one-dimensional, and usually are highly complex. The mother/daughter images for our times are deeply emotional representations that involve the passing on, and the discarding of traditions; the transition from childhood into womanhood in changing times; and the tensions and joys between differing personal and social realities. And yet, although motherhood/daughterhood changes, there is still a continual identity that is timeless.

My photographic journey into the lives of mothers and daughters began more than twelve years ago, and at its inception I was not able to articulate exactly why I was drawn to photographing this relationship. At the time, I was concerned with a lack of images of women as seen through the eyes of women. I felt a great need as a woman, and as an artist, to create images of women's lives and to share those with the world so that women could decide for themselves who they are and what they feel about themselves. Because women have always been presented with the oversimplified, blissful image of motherhood, and the mother/daughter relationship trivialized, we have become estranged from our own experience of this primary relationship that so profoundly shapes us.

As the project evolved, I realized that the reason I was photographing mothers and daughters was because of my own personal search for images of myself and my mother through the lives of other women. I thought that my own relationship with my mother was unusual because there often was a suffocating closeness as well as turbulence and drama. As I began to consciously separate from her, much anger arose, and with that anger, my guilt for feeling angry surfaced, which in turn spurred me on to keep examining through my photography how other mothers and daughters related. Over the years I have since found that my relationship with my mother was not uncommon, but followed lines similar to many mothers' and daughters' relationships. I began to realize that the conflicts that arise are a part of the process, and that openly acknowledging the conflicts, instead of hiding them, allowed for the necessary growth. I first photographed my mother and myself in 1974 as I began this project, and then again about ten years ago shortly after my father's death. The most recent photograph was taken in 1983 as my mother was packing for her move to Israel to begin a new life (p108). Although I still struggle with what the images reveal, I have grown tremendously since then in understanding and accepting my relationship with my mother.

I photographed family, friends, neighbors, strangers, and traveled to different parts of the United States looking for a wide variety of women who comprise the mothers and daughters of our society. My camera gave me license to step into the lives of so many people, and with little or no prompting, the story of their relationships began to unfold. I found that the universality of the mother/daughter bond cuts across all social, economic, and ethnic boundaries, and that there are basic ingredients, with fascinating variations, that go into this primary relationship. Frequently, the women I photographed were shocked at what was revealed in the images. It is rather difficult for many of us to look at images of ourselves, especially those that show pain, discord, wrinkles, or a surface numbness that covers potent emotions buried within. What often pleasantly surprised me were the instances when women would look at the photographs of themselves, feel vulnerable with what was revealed, and still give me permission to use those images. Many of these women also encouraged me to search further for more images that spoke to and helped women find the truths of their own relationships. Just the word *mother* would inevitably elicit a sigh or knowing nod, followed by women's stories of conflict, closeness, anger, confusion, love, encouragement—the whole gamut.

The relationship between mothers and daughters differs greatly from a woman's relationship with her son. It is taken for granted that sons will develop lives that are different than their mothers' lives. But daughters share not only the biological similarity of a female body, but the socio-political standing that our society accords women. Mothers and daughters tend to see each other as mirrors, therefore making the struggle for separation infinitely more difficult and often confusing. Women coming of age today face a very different set of expectations then those of past generations. A mother's lack of fulfillment, and a daughter's guilt for surpassing her, makes separation even more trying. In the past, a daughter would automatically inherit her mother's life roles, but today's women face options their mothers and grandmothers only dreamed about.

During the upheaval of the 1970's and the 1980's, psychologists and feminists have established the significance of a woman's relationship with her mother as she comes to terms with her own life. Poet-essayist Adrienne Rich calls the mother/daughter relationship "the great unwritten story." I wanted to tell that story through my photographs, to tell what passes between mothers and daughters. I wanted to capture the extreme closeness I saw in a mother and her child when the boundaries are blurred and inseparable. And the eventual need for the daughter to separate from her mother, a separation that usually begins in adolescence and continues for many women well into their adult lives. As the mothers and daughters age, there is either resolution of the relationship or an on-going ambivalence. The cycle com-

pletes itself with the daughter who cares for her elderly mother, or the relationship continues even after the mother or daughter has died. In addition to the basic ingredients of this relationship are the dramas that unfold making each relationship unique. There is the shared love and support; the mother and daughter that are strangers, yet fiercely connected by rage; the life of a single working mother; the daughter who breaks tradition; the cross-cultural and racial influences; the pull between tradition and modern ways; and the family dynamics of siblings and multi-generations. The intensities and the subtleties created by an emotional and physical bond are revealed through a posture, a sidelong glance, an article of clothing, or a twist of the head as well as by physical surroundings.

Women today are examining and reinterpreting their personal lives in relationship to themselves and to society. In turn, the mother/daughter relationship continues to change, no longer primarily concerned with teaching the traditional roles of wife and mother. Sometimes there is stony disapproval, even violent disagreement, across the generations. But also, there is great encouragement to go beyond the conventional definitions of "good" mothers and "dutiful" daughters, and to give each other support in creating alternatives to values that tend to limit women's lives. *A Portrait of American Mothers & Daughters* reflects upon this questioning and redefining by mothers and daughters, without judgment. These photographs are a straightforward, unmanicured look at a lifetime relationship, offering truthful images of mothers and daughters. As the truth is revealed, we can heal.

Raisa Fastman, 1987

A PORTRAIT OF AMERICAN
MOTHERS & DAUGHTERS

I had given birth to two sons. I dreamed of my girl-child, sure her soul was in contact with mine, awaiting entry to our world through me. I dreamed of her at sunset . . . on the beach . . . in Acapulco swinging lazily in a hammock with my mate. I dreamed of her in meditation with strong features, and her walk, a stride.

I birthed her; she birthed herself; we two together. Her father and her brothers were there with help, longing, and welcome. Her birth was the high arch of laughter.

Aviva Rahel and I are amazed and comforted by how our bodies fit, both when she lived within me and as she now lives, without. She is a source of liberation. For her brothers she inspires their paternal love and care. For her father she is much of him and all he will never be. For me, her mother, she is the continuation of the dream.

Nowadays, my daughter believes she makes all her own rules. I give her a lot and she seeks me out often, yearning for my arms and presence. She is four and beautiful. I have a grand piano. It is hard for Aviva Rahel to hear me when I say that I would like to play my piano. I insist that she respect my parameters, allowing me to be who I am and to do what I must do. I get really angry if I am interrupted when I am rehearsing or composing at the keyboard. I point out to her that ours is a household based on mutual respect and that I do not interrupt her when she is being creative.

The boundaries with a daughter are less clear. Aviva is at times imperious and at times sweet and spontaneous. She is even sweetly imperious! My desire is to always give her the space to create herself, and the tools for understanding herself and others in our complex world. Aviva Rahel speaks of the "heart seed" that makes her feel so warm. I have learned so much from my daughter. May she be blessed to carry her heart seed within her always.

Sheli Nan

Sheli Nan, 32, a musician and composer, with her two-month old daughter, Aviva Rahel Nan-Tabachnik, 1983.

Louise Jasper, 40,
executive secretary,
and Cristina Jasper,
3, 1986.

Donna Cummings, 27, homemaker, and Jacqueline Athena Dawn Cummings, 3, 1987.

My daughter is still very young. I delight in watching her growth, her enthusiasm for life, and her ever increasing self-awareness. At her present age of seven, she is happy with her female identity, and not the least bit timid about being feminine. In contrast, I grew up in a time and milieu which promoted a model of female deficit, powerlessness, suppression of talents, and passivity. When my baby turned out to be a daughter, my own apprehensions about the struggle to be a whole female person surfaced.

It is my dream that my daughter will grow so proud and secure in her female identity that when she discovers real world prejudices against women, she will be shocked (not threatened) because it is so laughable and inconsistent with her reality. I also hope she will be able to apply this insight to other types of prejudices she sees in her world. I would like her to appreciate the great continuum of people and their talents that make up our complex social world, and to believe that one grows and learns not just from birth to adulthood, but throughout one's life.

For my daughter and I, it is my dream that an open, loving, sharing relationship will always prevail over one with conflicts. When my daughter looks in a mirror in her adult life, I want her to see herself, but know she has had a mother who has loved and supported her.

Cheryl D. Dean

Cheryl D. Dean, 36,
graduate student in
clinical psychology,
and Megan Dean, 2,
1983.

Soge Track, 37, potter and writer, and Dakota Star, 6, 1987.

*Petra B. Salinas,
36, administrative
assistant, and
Angelica Reyna
Salinas, 9, 1986*

*Ann Howell-Isom,
30, nurse, and her
stepdaughter Robyn
Isom, 8, in an aban-
doned church, 1985.*

I traveled widely and taught writing for a number of years before Jessica was born. I was active in the civil rights movement and worked to end the war in Viet Nam, and was strongly influenced by the women's movement. I was surprised to discover sometime during Jessica's early years that having her had caused whatever commitments I had made to become deeper. I discovered that I wanted to create a world in which she would be able to grow up with dignity, feeling respected and loved, a world in which she would be able to work in accordance with her interests and abilities, wander where her feet and imagination would carry her. I want a world at peace without the threat of annihilation by war or hunger, a world that is green and healthy for my daughter.

Jessica is growing so beautifully towards womanhood! She comes home from school challenged and excited by ideas; I love the way her mind works, the way she analyzes thoughts and expresses herself. I love her moral outrage when she or others experience injustice, and the lilt of her laughter when something strikes her as funny. She has a terrific ear for languages and music, and when she plays her great-grandfather's violin the house is at peace, the way my childhood home was when my mother played the piano. She is the sort of person I want to know all of my/her life; she teaches me about myself.

What am I afraid of for my daughter? I know something about the levels of violence, both emotional and physical, that are inherent in a nation and a world dominated by men. If I feel a need to be cautious about expressing my thoughts and feelings, or cautious about contradicting the men with whom I work, and even with men I grow close to, how can I not be afraid for my daughter in her relationships with men? If I am afraid to walk alone in the night, how can I not be afraid for my young daughter as she crosses the city alone on her way to and from school? I am afraid that my daughter will be kidnapped or raped, broken in some way. I am also afraid that my daughter will learn to misstate her thoughts and disguise her feelings; that she will avoid certain activities and careers because of social values that may not, in truth, be relevant to her dreams and abilities. But of course my daughter's life is not mine, and my fears do not have to be her fears. While I try to make her aware of the dangers she might have to face, I also want her to live as free as possible from fear, to know that it's possible to walk alone and be safe, that it's possible to have warm and open relationships with men.

My advice to my daughter about being a mother would be to listen to your child. Your child will tell you from birth what she likes, doesn't like, needs and doesn't need. If you listen to her (or him), you will know when to step back out of the way for her growing; you will know when to part the waters so she can move on. You will remember your own childhood through her and learn about your own mother's mothering experience; you will learn about yourself.

Jeanne Angier

My mother and I get along very well. We have a special kind of friendship where we are both supportive of each other when it comes to just about everything. My mother is a strong person when it comes to many things. She has always taught me to do what I think is right, and I think that has helped me in a lot of ways. I know a few girls who are my age, whose mothers decide everything for them, but my mother lets me choose what I want to do and is very supportive of my decisions.

My mother grew up in a household where she was the oldest of seven children. She had to share a lot of her things and didn't get as much attention from her parents as she could have received. I, on the other hand, am an only child. I don't have to share my things with anyone else, and I get a lot of attention when I need it from my mother.

When my mother was growing up, most women stayed at home and cooked, cleaned, and cared for their children. Most women weren't encouraged to go out and get jobs, but were expected to mostly do what their husbands expected of them. When I was a little girl, my mother always explained to me that women's stereotypes could and should be overcome. She told me that just because I was a girl that didn't mean that I couldn't become a doctor or lawyer. She has always encouraged me to do what I want to do and not what other people tell me I have to do. Sometimes I wonder if my mother planned to only have one child, me, so that she could give me what she didn't get in her own childhood.

I know quite a few girls who don't have very good friendships with their own mothers. As I said before, I like the relationship that I have with my mother because we are both very supportive of each other. When either one of us has a problem, the other one tries to help out. If I have a problem at school, my mother is always there to support me on my decision or solution, or is there to give me suggestions.

I think that we complement each other in some ways. For example, I am not exactly the neatest person when it comes to keeping the house straightened, but my mother is always around to tell me to clean up after myself. My mother confides in me a lot and I try to show her that I care in return. Sometimes she might come home from work tired or upset, and so I usually go over to her and give her a hug to cheer her up because I really do care.

Jessica Angier

Jeanne Angier, 46,
language instructor,
and Jessica Angier,
10, wearing the cos-
tume her mother
made for her, 1983.

Ruth Pine Morgan,
40, photographer,
and Samantha
Morgan, 8, 1987.

One of the most important things I want to pass on to my daughter is the ability to get along with people and accept them for what they are. I treat people the way I want to be treated, so I try to be fair, and understanding of other people's feelings. Everybody's different, but we have to accept them for what they are . . . this is what my daughter's learning.

My grandmother raised me since I was three years old. My father used to beat up my mother . . . he was an alcoholic. He beat her up all the time, and one time they both made a dash for the pistol that they both knew was in the car. She got it first . . . and she shot him, and killed him. In some ways, I didn't understand that, and maybe it pushed me away from my mother. I was raised without a father and that was a little hard. But, now I'm beginning to understand her . . . I really feel my mother did what she had to do; it was self-defense. (She got out of jail right away.) My mother wanted to have me back and raise me when I was about 14, but I wanted to stay with my grandmother. Now, our relationship is getting a little better. I'm trying to dig inside myself and understand it. I see a lot of women going through being abused—just taking it and taking it, and not doing anything about it. That's how my mom was. My mom and I see each other about once a year. This last time we really talked, and she told me that's kind of how she felt. Back then, women didn't have much say in anything . . . they just took it. Now, it hurts me to see my friends go through that. I think they need to wake up and stand up for what they know is right . . . they don't need to be treated like that. It's wrong for a man to hit a woman, no matter what she's done. Women have other choices. They don't have to stay in relationships like that . . . life is too short as it is.

I see myself really trying to get close to my mom, but it's really hard. I've always been close to my grandmother. Every time I see my grandmother, she wants me to get close to my mother. We're both trying. I hope I don't have that kind of relationship with my daughter . . . I don't think I will because I've raised her and I know her . . . my mother didn't know me. Also, my daughter sees a lot of love in my relationship with my husband; we've been married for 15 years. My husband and I get along, we're able to talk, and there's a lot of love in the family. I hope my daughter finds love like I have, that's what I really wish for her. I want her to be happy . . . not like my two sisters who have a real hard life because they picked husbands just like my father. I did the exact opposite.

The advice I would give my daughter about being a mother is to go by the feelings that come from the heart, and not necessarily from books and other people.

Josie Sarabia

—My mother is nice to me and gives me lots of love.

—My mom brushes my hair too hard.

—My life has been different from my mother because she raised me, and her mom did not raise her.

—She helps me with my homework, and teaches me how to cook different foods.

—I am very happy with everything about my mother.

Jedi Sarabia

Josie D. Sarabia,
34, housekeeper,
and Jedi Sarabia,
8, in backyard with
tepee used for ritu-
als in the Native
American Church.

Frances S. Montaya,
41, homemaker;
Georgia Romero,
23, homemaker,
and her daughter
Sarah Romero, 8,
1987.

My hopes for my daughter are many: that she continues to grow toward self-understanding and independence; that she retains her health and sense of humor; and that the care and sensitivity she has for others do not diminish. My greatest fear is of the many external dangers in the world: physical/sexual assault; the threat of nuclear war and therefore, no future; child snatching; traffic collisions; and the high risk of injury or death.

I am most proud of Talia's ability toward introspection of herself and others. Her insight, creative initiative, and curiosity to learn about the world is a continual reminder to me of how much I learn from her about living. Her spectacular artwork is a constant joy and source of pride to me.

If I were to start over again as a mother, I would change several techniques and attitudes regarding mothering, running a household, and parenting with her dad, my husband. I would be more relaxed, of course, because I would trust the limits of my physical and emotional stamina and fortitude, and I'd be more confident of my abilities. Most significantly, I would give to myself more by pursuing self-fulfilling activities and recreation as a way of replenishing and nurturing myself. Motherhood is such a tremendous responsibility, stress, and drain, and the highs and lows such extremes, that I often found myself at the point of exhaustion too many times. My own self-esteem should have been more of a priority; to keep it on an uphill course, no matter how long it took. There were times I thought I would go crazy trying to be what I thought everyone wanted, and times when I *was* crazy because I was attempting to live up to my *own* unrealistic standards—Marabel Morgan one day, Gloria Steinem the next.

I am 42 now, and those experiences happened when Talia was born and several years thereafter. The glare of what was really happening during that time—growth—continues to shine brightly in my mind. I feel such strong empathy for other women struggling through the maze of feelings, the physical and mental fatigue that saturates to the bone, the demands, and often hopelessness of the irreversible situation of being a *mother*. The results, growth, skills, and opportunities I received from the experience of being a mother were often obscured and out of perspective until much later on . . . sometimes years.

For me, motherhood developed strengths I never knew I had; it solidified my integrity; pushed me over the edge and showed me another side of myself; threw me into the horror of knowing what a thin line child abuse is; and from the depths of grief, distress and worry, I experienced rising to the pure ecstasy and joy at the first step or first word of my baby.

My advice to Talia about being a mother is that motherhood is a time for the unique possibility of:
—Feeling, smelling, touching, tasting, and seeing the miracle of birth.
—Watching and caring for an infant person, experiencing the growth process.
—Being physically and emotionally pushed to new limits.
—An opportunity to feel the experiences our own mothers went through sensing the difficulty, joy, pain, frustration, pride, rage, excitement, and laughter.
—Exploration of ourselves so completely that, hopefully, we emerge more mature and more fully aware of how continuing the growth process is, and how much we have to look forward to.
—Learning to trust, pray, and be confident in ourselves that our children will be safe, healthy, and our parenting effective.
—Comprehending what it means being without a thank you, a hug or appreciation when it is needed the most. When your child says, "I hate you," to feel the blow of the words and feelings, and respond honestly and objectively to the child's age level.
—Accepting the feelings that confuse, anger, and frustrate; to know that these are what we all feel, and that these feelings reflect a process of growing and searching . . . that to deny or repress them is to miss understanding a very important part of ourselves.

I would gladly give practical advice to my daughter to help ease the frustrating newness of the situation; but I hope I will also know when not to say *anything,* remembering that moving through a learning process has times when just nonverbal, loving support is most needed . . . letting her have the pleasure of solving new problems, or designing a new way to do something, or pushing herself to find support with other mothers, dealing with the frustration, and just plain learning how to accept and live with it . . . because it doesn't end!

Jennifer Lovell Scherquist

Jennifer Lovell Scherquist, 40, day care administrator and artist, and Talia Scherquist, 9, 1985.

Holit Bat-Edit, 39,
businesswoman,
and Tali Klein, 12,
1982.

Lorene Warwick,
44, photographer;
Jessica Diurni,
12; and Summer
Warwick, 6, 1984.

I was going to write the definitive sermon on mothering, but I realized that there is very little to say about motherhood that is definitive—not if what you have to say is real and honest. What we have always known about Mother is that whether she is short or tall, rich or poor, black or white, fat or thin, mother of one or of many, Mother was praiseworthy in terms of the many sacrifices she made for her family. If there wasn't enough pie for everyone, suddenly, Mother wasn't very hungry. Mother always took the smallest pork chop, the chipped plate. It was Mother who scrimped and scraped so her daughter could have a new dress for graduation or her son a new baseball glove.

It is true that the institution of motherhood has been altered in some ways. Today, women are still to become mothers in order to fulfill the cultural ideal, but they are to do so with seemingly less fervor, less single-mindedness. Now, they are to combine motherhood with occupation and do both simultaneously. But actually, the underlying messages have not changed very much: to be kind, nurturing, selfless; to accommodate, and despite other conflicts and obligations, always put her children first and be there when she is needed. The expectations of motherhood are so overwhelmingly unrealistic, that even those of us who have enjoyed the fullest sort of mothering are somehow failed by our mothers. And those of us who set out to be mothers, know that at some level, we are doomed to failure.

Fearfulness seems to be a requisite for mothering. Even if we have grown to scorn the fears of our mothers with which we were raised, we are somehow bidden to construct another set of fears by which to raise our own children. As a stepmother, I struggle daily with my own doubts. Am I being too tough and demanding when I insist that we confront one another and try to reach some mutual understanding? Do the pressures and demands of my professional life rob my stepdaughters of their right to my undistracted ear and the sense that I am there for them? In my indignation at the cultural stereotypes, do I present them with an impossible, disconsonant role model? Will I smother them with my own fearfulness? Or will I bruise them with my insistence that the world is their oyster and they must sally forth and seize it? The only guarantee is that I will not do it entirely right, and this will probably be the source of recriminations when they are grown.

Mothering also moves in other directions. Not all of us are destined to experience biological motherhood. However, many of us will, and through that experience we may come to broaden and deepen our experience of ourselves and the times in which we live. But we all have the experience of confronting our mothers. Be they present or absent, living or dead, they are figures with which each of us is destined to grapple. For many women of my generation, that confrontation brings us to an understanding of how we have struggled to create identities *different* from those of our mothers. Virtually all of us devote at least a significant part of our adult lives attempting to resolve and understand that critical relationship. "Scanning one another like unfinished murder mysteries, unable to let go of one another," as Nancy Friday has described it.

There is inevitably a phase of the relationship between mother and adult daughter which is a process of mutual forgiveness and pardon—each to the other—for all the imperceptible wounds inflicted over the years. Daughters forgiving mothers for closing them out. Mothers forgiving daughters for achieving too easily what they had to forfeit. Forgiving mothers for not protecting daughters from what they have chosen not to see. And hoping, at the same time, that mothers will be able to forgive daughters for those things they did not know. Mothers and daughters . . . what a profound ambivalence there is . . . the confusion of otherness and identity.

At the best of times we mothers are a wonder; warm, fun, funny, stunning in our glamour, generous, and wise. At our worst, we are self-contradictory, stingy, rigid. Even as adults, we sometimes catch ourselves calling for "mommy." As if mommies could really soothe and erase the pain and fear and make everything better, just the way they were once able to do when we believed in their omniscience, their eternal and unconditional love and power. The relationship between mother and daughter is central to the formation of a woman's image of herself. Exploring the relationship between mother and daughter forces a woman to plumb the deepest levels of her experience. For many of us who are now adult, that exploration has led beyond our biological mothers into intimate and profoundly caring relationships with women other than our mothers, women with whom this exploration of self and others can take place in a less defended, less prickly, more open arena.

We are learning to mother one another in the best sense of the word. We are learning to use mother as a verb, rather than only as a noun. But in order to get to that truly nurturing place, we must cast aside many of the stereotypical notions of mother . . . most specifically, we must cast off "mother, the eternally self-sacrificing." For ourselves and for our children, we must refuse to be victims. We must develop a profound kind of loving that transcends the saccharine pap of the old cultural ideal of mother. The most important legacy a mother can leave her children is the quality of her own life. The quality of the mother's life can be enhanced, not by sentiments and sweets, but by confirming and supporting her reality as a mother, as a woman, as a full-fledged human being.

Joan Hull

31

Landes Good, 37,
fundraiser, and Teal
Good, 10, 1984.

Toby Lerner Ansin,
46, ballet and arts
advocate, and
Stephanie Lerner
Ansin, 15, 1987

My daughter has been studying ballet with me since birth. I realize now at her young age of 12 that her dedication toward ballet is more than I could have ever hoped she would have toward any profession. So now my hopes for her are probably her hopes. The high degree of commitment required from a young adolescent is at times overwhelming. I hope the career my daughter has chosen will be as rewarding and fulfilling a part of her life as mine is. Our fields being the same, we share the same hopes: hoping the body stays slim; hoping for daily improvement in technique; hoping injuries will not plague her; hoping she will be selected for the best parts; hoping she will never have an off performance; and of course, hoping she gets the job and role she is dreaming of. I truly love that we are sharing these same aspirations, and since I've been in the same career, I want to ease her way in it. Knowing that may not be possible, I hope she has the security and strength of character to withstand all the difficulties ahead and achieve her goals.

Besides success in her career, I have another set of hopes for my daughter; funny how I remember these were the hopes my mother had for me. A career is wonderful, but can be lonely. The ultimate fulfillment for any person is not found in personal victory, but in commitment to others. The joy and satisfaction my career gave me pale compared to the joy and satisfaction my daughter's career gives me. I hope she one day will have the opportunity to experience this higher level of joy. Since I am her ballet teacher and we work together four to five hours a day, my daughter and I are as one. I have no fears about her going astray, she has shown too many years of self-dedication. She has proven to me over and over again she knows that in order to excel, she must continually work to improve herself. My biggest fear is how each of us will cope with a prolonged physical separation.

I am very proud of my daughter's accomplishments and she is everything I could have ever wanted. She is constantly trying to please me and I often try to be more like her. I secretly hope I was as kind and gentle to my own mother when she was alive as my daughter is to me now. She often surprises me with breakfast in bed, a late snack, a clean kitchen, doing the laundry— all with the same answer that she thinks I work too hard. I don't think we have ever had a real fight. Oh yes, before ballet performances we are at each other's throats because we get nervous for each other. But after the performances we always have a good laugh at the fools we were! I have only one disappointment in life about my daughter, and that is the fact that my mother never saw this wonderful continuity of life. I am always thinking about how thrilled and elated she would have been with us, and how much my daughter and I are missing out in not having my mother around us.

Carol Ravich

My mother is a ballerina and has danced professionally almost all of her life. That is exactly what I want to do. I don't know if I ever would have had a ballet class if she weren't my mother, and I had a mother who was a lawyer. I love ballet, and I hate to think how it would have been if I had never been given ballet. The most positive thing my mother has done for me is to give me the love for ballet and the kind of training I need in order to succeed. She has also given me life.

The most difficult part of my relationship with my mother is leaving her for school every day. I do well in school, but I can't stand to be away from her for so many hours. I know I must sound like a six-year-old, but I am always thinking that when she is away from me she could get hurt, and I won't be with her. I have no regrets or disappointments as a daughter. I love my mother more than anyone could love anyone in the whole world. I am never angry more than five minutes, and then it's just about stupid problems like when I am reminded to do something, or wear a certain dress. I very quickly realize she's right and it's dumb to stay mad.

I feel my life has been the same as my mother's. I think I am given the same things my mother got when she was my age. Also, it is kind of neat that I love the same things my mother does. The only real difference is my mother didn't cook as much as I do and that is because she didn't have a microwave oven when she was my age.

I am pleased that my mother runs a ballet school where I can study all the time. My mother keeps herself in such good shape compared to all my other friends' mothers, and I am so proud to be seen with her. I am pleased with myself as the daughter because I know that I am making my mother very happy when I work hard. I love how she kisses and hugs me when I surprise her by cleaning the house. I want to be able to make everything all right, the way my mother can, and I want her energy.

Heather Ravich Goldstein

*Carol Ravich, balle-
rina, and Heather
Ravich Goldstein,
12, 1987*

Lynn Bilik, 43, social worker, and Jen Bilik, 16, student, 1985.

*Yael Lurie
Larochette, 40,
painter and de-
signer, and Yadin
Larochette, 14, 1983.*

Susan Griffin, 41,
writer, and Chloe
Levy, 15, 1984.

Martha Cochrane, 41, teacher and counselor; Julie Tugend, 17; and Katherine Tugend, 14, posing in their wonder women outfits for a family skit, 1979. Julie is now a political aide and Katherine is an administrative assistant.

The hopes I have for my daughter are openness to change and the ability to love and accept herself. I fear that she will not be at peace with herself and there will not be peace in the world.

I am proud that my daughter has grown into a beautiful, strong woman who knows how to take care of herself and feels free to be who she is. Becky has never disappointed me. When problems come up we have always been able to talk it out. How can I have disappointments in a child who tried so hard to bring her mother up as well as herself? She has always been hard on herself and I would like her to be able to relax more with life.

If I had to do it over again, I would make a conscious choice and raise her with more awareness. Also, I would have played with her more and taught her how to play and have fun. I passed on to Becky a sense of self and independence that I worked so hard to get for myself while she was growing up . . . a caring for people and a willingness to put a lot of energy into helping others.

I've gotten a sense of family from being a mother. This is important to me. Ever since my mother and aunt died, I've not really had much connection with my father and brothers. I have learned how to let go, and what unconditional love means, and maybe to forgive my parents.

Advice is something my daughter doesn't want unless she asks for it. About being a mother? What do I know? This person brought up herself. I was her vehicle into the world and supplied her survival needs, which included a lot of "lovies and huggies"—she did the rest.

At 21 years old, my daughter is making a conscious decision not to have a child herself—she may change her mind. Whatever she does, it will be a conscious decision made with awareness of the options and alternatives. This is what I wanted to see happen for the next generation of women. This is what we worked for in the consciousness raising groups, women's centers, the marches and demonstrations during the 60s and 70s. If only my daughter makes a conscious decision about having a child, it will all be worth it.

Suzanne Lane

My mother has always been a positive influence on my life. I guess the most positive thing she has given for me so far in her life is her constant support and love. She is always straightforward and honest. She has taught me to know how I feel and to be honest with myself about those feelings.

The most difficult part of my relationship with my mother is sometimes wanting her to not react as a mother. To just be a friend and listen without feeling like she has to offer advice and wisdom. I'm most angry about not being able to be a kid during a lot of the time I was growing up. Feeling a lot of responsibility to take care of myself and my mother. My life has been extremely different from my mother's. Being raised by a single, lesbian mother is at the other end of the spectrum in comparison to my mother, who was raised by two parents in the 1950's with two brothers and a large extended family.

My mother is nonjudgmental of me and I'm pleased that no matter what I do, I know she will always love me. As the daughter, I'm pleased that I have the ability to know how I feel and be honest about that. I think I'm a strong person. I would like to have the job security my mother has as a nurse, and some of her wisdom that probably comes with age. I would like less "hips" and maybe less struggle and difficulties in my life. It is a difficult task for me to pick out specifics about my mother. I can't put limits on a mother/daughter relationship because there are no extremes, it's everything in between.

Becky Knickerbocker

Suzanne Lane, 45, registered nurse, and Becky Knicker-bocker, 17, sales clerk, 1983.

41

Loni Hancock, 46,
mayor of Berkeley,
California; Leita
Hancock, 21, stu-
dent (right); and
Mara Hancock, 19,
student, 1983.

Pat Schroeder, 46, U.S. Congresswoman, and Jamie Schroeder, 16, public high school student, 1987.

The loss of a lover is familiar, the rejection
is painful, yet predictable.

You left me, and I felt abandoned
and displaced.
Knowing that all these years
that you would one day leave me
did not make it any easier, and
wanting you to leave, left my heart aching.
But Geminis and mothers
are skilled at double binds.

There were no bitter words, no anger, no tears.
It would have been easier
had there been a dramatic exit,
a cry for freedom, a plea for independence.
But it was your
necessary rite of passage
and came as no surprise;
But loss is something you can never prepare for,
Even if it is done in soft stages.

I wanted the event of your leaving
to be more comfortable
than the occassion of your birth;
I wanted it all to be so right.
So many stories I never shared with you . . .
All of the songs I never sang with you;
Wanting to arm you for your journey
away from me, but feeling I released you
to their world unprepared.

The guilt of not providing the perfect life
for you, rises to the surface
like dead leaves in a pond;
All of the times that I said "yes" to lovers
and "no" to you;
All of the time I carefully processed
and still made the wrong choices;
All of the times I heard my own conclusions
as you tried to explain yourself to me;
All of the misplaced anger
that I could give only you;
All of the times I blamed you,
because I stopped dreaming
and refused to grow.

But I did kiss you in the night
and chased away your nightmares;
and I made up stories and songs
that made you laugh full and strong,
and most times, I was there for you
and recognized, most clearly
that facing you is facing me.

And I encouraged you to claim your life
and fight like hell for your right to be;
and the best gift that I could ever give
to you
was to say "yes" to your dreams
that were not my own.

Margaret Sloan-Hunter 1986

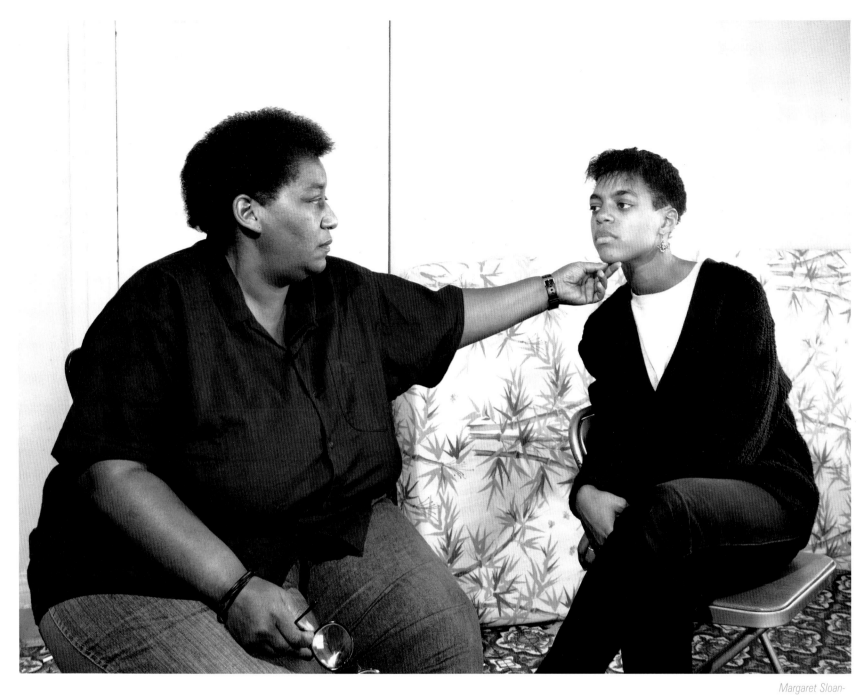

Margaret Sloan-Hunter, 39, writer, and Katherine Sloan, 19, 1986.

Mani Terry
Fenniger, 42,
sales manager
and personal con-
sultant, and Sarah
Berger, 16, 1987.

Merle Woo, 40, social feminist educator, and Emily Woo Yamasaki, 19, actress and clerical worker, 1982.

Jacquie Stevens,
38, potter, and Kelly
L. Webster, 17,
1987.

Pat Norman, 37, political activist and feminist therapist; Elise Norman, 16, and Angela Norman, 13, 1977. Elise is now a teacher and entrepreneur, and Angela is a college student and businesswoman.

My Darling Stephanie,

I was asked to write about our relationship to accompany our photograph, but when I tried to just write about us, it became too emotional. Then I decided to try writing it all out in a letter to you.

It would be so easy to sum us up with a simple "I love you and you love me" because that is, after all, the case of this life we share. But it leaves so much unsaid.

It doesn't describe the pain we've felt or the acceptance we've had to make. Not over the fact that you're retarded, but pain because for some reason God must have felt there was more we needed to deal with. Big deal, you learn slower, and some things like calculus and understanding why Halley's Comet appears so seldom will never be possible for you. Such are the trade-offs in life. No matter how hard I try, I cannot make sense out of the pain and fear your many recent illnesses have caused you. I see the pain and another part of my heart dies and is replaced by an ache that remains—nothing takes it away, not even the incredible joy you bring me.

I've tried so hard to always be honest with you. But there are times when I feel like I'm cheating you. You ask me, "Why did I have to have so many strokes? Why don't my seizures stop? Why doesn't the pain go away?" I can only answer, "I don't know." I would give my life to make it all better, honey, but I can't. I can only promise to be there for you always. Whatever happens, we'll deal with it together.

If there are times when I seem sad, know that it's nothing you've done. Sometimes I think of the things you've missed; having a boyfriend, your first kiss, driving a car, your senior prom, getting married and having a child of your own. I've wanted all of these for you. It saddens me that you'll never experience them. It also saddens me that I will never be a grandmother. Oh, how I would have loved that. Now it's just another aching spot in my heart.

Don't misunderstand me. I'm not complaining. You've given me more love and joy than most mothers and daughters ever share. I'd do it all again just for the honor and the wonder of being *your* mother. You've taught me so much about self-growth, and you've shown me that no matter how tough or dark times seem to be, you'll always find a way to cope. I admire your strength so much; I draw all of mine from you.

I love you,

Mom

Lyndene Ginsburg,
38, teacher's
assistant, and
Stephanie Andrews,
19, student, 1987.

Mamie Williams,
70, retired business
owner; Joyce
Martin, 46, busi-
ness owner; and
Ilana Martin, 15,
student and aspir-
ing singer, 1986.

Niety Gerson, wife and mother, and Pamela Segal, 23, bank management, 1987.

My hopes for Erika are that she will feel fulfillment with her own sense of creativity as an artist, and know that she has power as a valuable person with choices in the world. I trust that she knows herself and is in touch with her feelings. She is extremely self-sufficient and independent, and takes care of herself financially. Sometimes I worry if she is too responsible. In the past, our life was unstable financially because her stepfather is a musician, and only recently have I begun to earn money as an actress. I wish I had been able to give her more financially all those years when we were struggling. There was emotional stress along with the financial instability, and lots of times I was too much for Erika. I needed a lot of mothering myself because I grew up in foster homes, and I did not get nurturing from my parents and felt extremely abandoned. So, as a mother, I was carrying a lot of these needs, and under stress, the boundaries got fuzzy and I was demanding that Erika mother me when she was the one who needed a mother. But I was always aware and involved in therapy or ways to work on our problems with guidance, which was not the case with my parents.

I know as a child I felt I was a bad person because my family left me. I wanted Erika never to have to feel like a bad person for any reason or because of what we adults did. From the beginning, I honored her sense of insightfulness and felt that, even as a child, she knew best about her own feelings. I broke a lot of patterns from my past generation, and learned how to view a person or child as an individual and not an extension of the parents to be controlled. This was very exciting as Erika really led me through a transformation of values in the 1960's and 1970's that the whole country was going through . . . a breakdown of authority. I feel so lucky that I got to experience this with her, and that she emerged less fearful about the world and free of many problems I have.

The roughest period for us was the separation stage. It brought up all my fears of being left. I had to let go of what defined a large part of my identity—being her mother. She needed to resent me and react to me in a negative way in order to carve out her own identity, separate from me. It's funny, because I remember fighting about clothes a lot. I see our passage related to this. First, she didn't like my clothes, then she took them all. I would want things back as I felt deprived and left, and even jealous. Now, I'm trying to give them to her. We went through this dance a lot. In the process of mothering, I was also able to mother myself by loving Erika. I feel I am more whole and healed by being able to care for someone this intimately. It is an amazing challenge to stay in touch with the precarious balance of identities between mother and daughter. We are good friends now, and have established our own identities.

Tina Preston

My relationship with my mother is very special to me. As well as being mother and daughter, we share a friendship that is close and active. Our strong relationship has grown out of her constant support and acceptance of me as an individual. She has given me the freedom to make my choices, encouraging me to grow. I think this is the base, because I don't feel restricted by her or her values, or that I need to conform to them in order for us to relate. This makes our friendship sincere. I know deep down that whatever I go through, my mother is there and loves and accepts me.

Looking back on our relationship, as a daughter I always had this idea that we were equal—or should be. I was quite headstrong in this way, which created a lot of conflicts because I would not compromise. I have no idea where I got this idea about mother/daughter equality at 13 years old. I think we all feel this way. She did not suppress it, but instead she encouraged me to speak out and make many of my own choices. This made me feel equal. I never felt overpowered or threatened by her "authority."

The most difficult part of our relationship is dealing with my mother when she is under heavy stress. I react to her badly when I'm put in the position of listener or mediator—and she feels unsupported, and we end up in a situation where we both feel defeated. This is very difficult and painful for me, and makes me feel helpless. I'd like to help her, but can only go so far. Her stress is so much heavier than mine, and maybe I'm not equipped to deal with it. Sometimes, I would like a little less of her concern—this may sound ridiculous—and maybe a little less friendship. There are times when I become hostile and show anger for years of listening to her disappointments in life, which hurts and frustrates me because I want her to be happy, and I'm always stuck with the feeling that she is schlepping her problems onto me, which I can't sort out. Sometimes I feel that she is using me for the scapegoat, and whether or not this is real or my reaction, the situation is yet to be resolved.

We have a special relationship because it is based on honesty and openness. We share many of the same interests and circles of friends. I think this is a good bond, but sometimes, I feel it's too close for my own growth. I feel that I should move away and stamp out my own ground because we, as young adults, are led to believe this. And we are expected to rebel against our parents' lifestyle. I fight with this idea—on the one hand, I think it's imperative that I do this, and on the other hand, I can't see anything that I need to run from. Our relationship is still growing and changing, and I think it will take on a new light after my mother reads this . . . .

Erika Bradberry

Tina Preston, 45, actress, and Erika Bradberry, 21, student, 1985.

To be a mother is to feel love from the inner depths of your heart; and to be the mother of a daughter creates a bond that grows as time goes by. From the very beginning, I wanted my daughter to enjoy learning because this was one of the greatest gifts my parents gave to me. Because Leila was a gifted child, I have felt a stronger sense of responsibility towards her in giving her the opportunity to expand in knowledge and self. Also, to be an individual with compassion, love, a positive outlook, and patience. My heritage has given me strength and values to focus on, and I hope Leila has been able to absorb some of the culture from me.

I am Mexican and my husband is Iranian. I suppose the traditional role I grew up with in terms of being a woman has been a problem for me, and I tried not to impose that on my daughter. My husband always tried to get me to make more decisions early on in our marriage. However, my father was very traditional, and he was the head of the household. He always had the first and final word. I've changed so much in the last ten years. I'm a lot more sure of myself. I know I've learned to recognize my capabilities, and this has made me feel a whole lot better and more assured of what I do in my life. I'm hoping that my daughter will see me as a stronger person, and that my husband and I are more equal in the role of raising the kids, and dealing with everyday life. And that, even though I'm home, I'm contributing a lot. The only thing I think I'd do differently is to come across stronger. I don't think I come across to my daughter as a real strong person, and I know that has made her not stand up for her own rights or ideas. That was more apparent when she was smaller, but now she is much more sure of herself. To me, that was a direct consequence of my own insecurities that I felt.

Leila has a strong personality and is a very moody person. It's difficult to deal with her moods, especially with her father. I think I understand her moods better than her father, and I kind of smooth out the relationship. Leila expresses her opinions or viewpoint, but it was different when I was growing up . . . I couldn't do that. I was brought up to respect my parents all the time. So, any time I had a difference of opinion, I always had to keep quiet, especially with my father. With my mom, I was a little more open. I don't want to hinder Leila from expressing her opinions to her father, but some times the most difficult part is smoothing over the relationship between them. I just want to make sure that Leila sticks up for herself because I always had a difficult time doing that.

Even though we are mother and daughter, we are very individual. Leila is my daughter, but she's my friend too. It has

been my wish that her life be easier than mine, and just as rich. For Leila's future, I hope she will be happy, and that she be blessed with a daughter of her own.

Rosalinda Astarai

My mother and I have many differences, now, much more than we used to when I lived at home. I don't know if they're for better or for worse, but there are some things between us that will never change. There is a respect for her that I have had ever since I can remember, and I still have it, although I'm more outspoken with her than I was as a child. One thing a university teaches you is to challenge concepts and ideas that are thought to be taken as standard, and to exert one's own opinion. One learns to become more independent in the way that one thinks because parents are no longer there to give you input all the time. Helpful advice comes from peers, which I never take to heart as much as I would my mother's advice.

When I was a young child, I had doubts as to my mother's love for me, as I think most children do. But now, I know her love is real, and my love for her is real and eternal too. Also, I am an adult now, and our relationship can be a more equal one. I no longer need the protection of her love to get me through my daily events. Yet, I can't do without it either.

Our lifestyles are obviously very different, but my life compared with my mother's life when she was my age is even more different. I'll be 21 years old soon, and my mom gave birth to me when she was about that age. She was married at 20, and I'm still in school, and possibly going to graduate school after I get my engineering degree.

My relationship with my mom is definitely a subtle one. I only see her two or three times a month now, and we seem to have many differences. But these factors have never detracted from our relationship—they may yet be another proving ground for it. It's an unspoken, unquestioned relationship that has evolved from a purely dependent role on my part to a fully interactive relationship. My love for her runs deep, and remains mostly unspoken, but it is there in strength. I like to think I am independent of her sometimes, but I know that my independent life here runs smoothly because I know she is supportive of my efforts as a student. If her approval and support were ever withdrawn, my foundation would be yanked from underneath me—but this would never happen.

Leila Astarai

Rosalinda Mejia
Astarai, 42, home-
maker in transition,
and Leila Astarai,
20, engineering stu-
dent, 1987.

Eleanor Cutri Smeal,
47, President of the
National Organiza-
tion for Women,
and Lori Ann Smeal,
19, college student,
1987.

Daphne Innes, 47, computer scientist, and Mary Innes, 25, general contractor, 1982.

We are living at a moment when the climate of social sympathies in this country of freedom makes us, as women, most unique in the history of mankind. Never before have elements existed to make it possible for us to express oursleves in so many ways in addition to motherhood.

The result is a very different motherhood than that of our past or even of our present sisters in other less progressive countries. Our hopes and fears are more pronounced since we know that our daughters are entering a stage set by the pioneers of this generation of "super moms." What the result of the opened pathways lying before these bright unlimited children will bring is exciting to contemplate and as adventurous as exploring the moon. At last, the gifts, talents and minds of generations of women will be free to fly, to explore, to express. Mothers and daughters can share this special experience. They are opening together the unlimited vistas to the future.

My life bridges the past and the future with both my mother and my daughter. To experience one who baked all her own bread, or felt unworthy, and see another vie for president and CEO of a Fortune 500 company and feel unworthy, is an astonishing experience that I could never have without both being and having a wonderful mother and daughter. The most creative and meaningful accomplishment in my life is to have this daughter who loves, understands and respects me and gives my life real meaning. Yet, my wish for her is as old fashioned as can be; health, happiness, peace, love and a daughter for her as wonderful as she has been for me.

Lynn Wilson Spohrer

It was not until I returned from my freshmen year in college that I realized how close the tie is between my mother and I. I was always close to her throughout my life; it was a kind of closeness where I felt that I could tell her anything, but I only did this when I really needed to. We never spent a lot of time together because we were both always busy. She was putting most of her efforts into her business, while I was dancing, cheerleading, or playing sports. I also think that I was too young to understand that which is so special between us.

Although the circumstances of our lives have been very different, the more we talk the more I realize how similar we are. She had many more hardships as a youngster than I did. She had to work throughout her teenage years, whereas I only spend summers working. I have been given a lot, not an excessive amount, but enough where I have been grateful and happy. I haven't taken advantage; I strive and work for what I want. I definitely inherited this system of values from my mother.

I think the most difficult part of our relationship was during the time of her divorce. At the time, I didn't understand why she left because I was too young, and I think I held it against her for awhile. But now I realize and understand the reasons why. I guess it made me stronger because I realized how strong she was.

The biggest influence my mother has had on me is simply herself. I don't know how to put it any other way. I have learned so much from her. I have seen her accomplishments through her hard work and this desire has been passed on to me. It was nothing that I did consciously; I didn't try to emulate her, it just happened with certain things. For example, I have always been a hard working and dedicated student, and so was my mother . . . It wasn't that we were both naturally brilliant, but we always made better grades by putting a lot more effort into things than did the person with the same amount of intelligence. There must be some reason why I share many of her same qualities and mannerisms. I think there is some hidden link between mothers and daughters, and I feel there is a particularly strong one between my mother and I.

We're not so similar because we spent so much time together because we didn't. I never knew the many things that we shared until I had already developed them myself, and realized the similarities when I was about 18 years old. I feel very close to her because we have so much in common, not just because she is my mother. But we're not exactly the same, I'm sure we differ in some aspects. Of course, a lot of people could say they're very similar to other people. Everyone is tied to someone, especially their mother. I have never met anyone but my mother with as similar values and opinions as mine.

Alysia Wilson

Lynn Wilson Spohrer, 45, president and chief executive officer of her own company in hotel interior design and architecture, and Alysia Wilson, 19, student, 1987.

61

On the day Alison was born, I couldn't believe the richness of my blessing. Twenty-four years later as a mother of three daughters, I feel triply blessed. I enjoy being a mother, especially a mother of daughters.

My dream for Alison is that her life be happy, that she live the life she wants for herself, and have the opportunity to love and be loved to the fullest. When she was very young, I worried about the pain of a skinned knee, a broken balloon, or the loss of a dropped ice cream cone. Today, I still worry about the figurative skinned knee, not because I see it as inevitable, but rather because I would always like to shield my daughters from anything that might hurt. The hardest part of being a mother is allowing children to grow up in the real world and experience all that life has to offer—good and bad.

Alison is gentle, trusting, tolerant and compassionate. She has a quietness and evenness which allow her to accept without censorship, and experience without wild mood swings. She is accommodating, perhaps often in the extreme, so that at times her own opinions may be buried under the more forcefully stated thoughts of others. I would like to see her develop enough confidence, as I think she is beginning to do, so she can accept the value of her own ideas and be assertive without feeling defiant.

When my daughter contemplates motherhood, I would suggest the thought that I lived with as my own daughters were growing. We pass this way only once, so *enjoy*. Take time to be a part of your children's lives, but allow them the freedom to develop as unique individuals. Children do not always opt for their parents' choices, but if their decisions are not destructive, I would counsel acceptance. Decide what is important enough to argue over, and ignore the unimportant, allowing room for growth and friendship in your relationship.

I am pleased and proud that Alison is my daughter and that I can be her friend. I am sorry that it is easier to be better friends when we have distance between us, but I see changes as the bride is becoming the wife. When the couple become parents, I think the metamorphosis will be complete. Then I believe she will feel and accept her equal adult status with me as her mother and friend.

Beryl K. Smith

My mother has given me love, support, encouragement, understanding, and her abounding generosity. I learned a powerful lesson from my mother in my late teen years as I watched her go back to college at middle age to complete her college and graduate work. I learned from her the importance of making sure I could always rely upon myself. This motivated me to continue my education through college and graduate school at an early age.

I would have liked a little more freedom as a teenager; to be able to fall down, possibly, instead of being restricted from things my mother disapproved of. I have noticed that my mother became much freer with my younger sisters as they passed through their teenage years. I regret that it never seemed okay for me to be angry. Now, I regret that we live so far apart from each other and do not see each other much except at holidays and occasional visits. But she has always been available to me, even though we have lived two to three thousand miles apart for the last three-and-a-half years.

My life has been different from my mother's in that her life was more limited and conservative when she was my age. I have been raised in a society where there are more acceptable roles for women and more choices. I also received much more support and encouragement from my mother to pursue my goals than she did from her mother. I believe that I had a much happier childhood than my mother due to the quality of her and my father as parents.

My mother is a fun person who loves to plan and do things. She has given me great exposure to culture, encompassing theatre, ballet, music, art and travelling. I was given numerous opportunities to pursue interests as a kid, whether it was dance lessons, water ballet, gymnastics, piano, art, or summer camp. My mother devoted so much of her time and energy towards me and my sisters when we were children, and spent private time with each of us. She is witty and intelligent, and kind to other people. I admire these qualities, and would like to have more of my mother's friendliness, spunk, and guts to stick up for myself. I have always strived to please both my mother and father. I feel that I communicate well with my mother, and believe that she is proud of my academic achievements, my new marriage, and that I am a good person.

Alison M. Acton

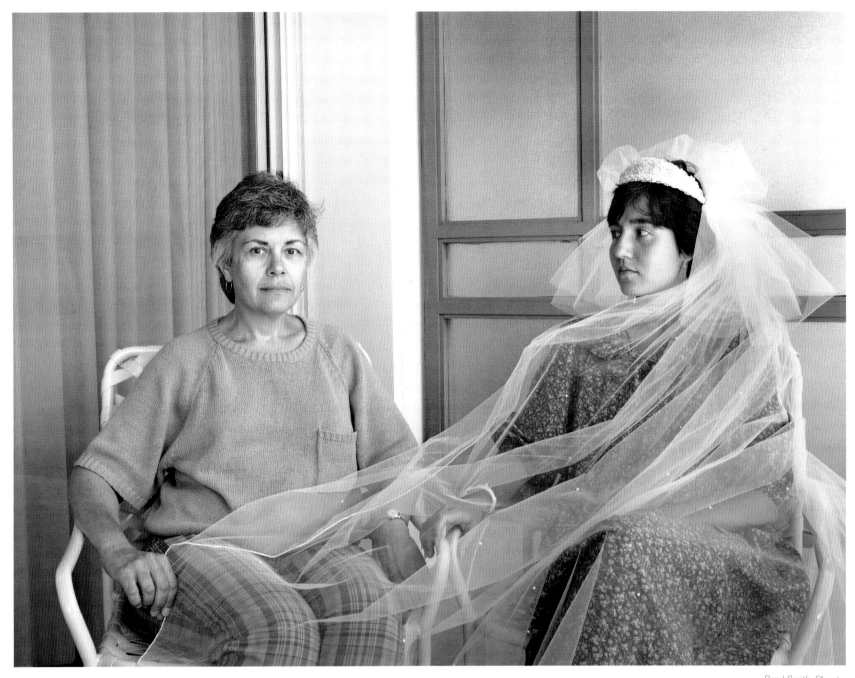

Beryl Smith, 51, art librarian, and Alison Acton, 23, marriage, family and child counselor, the day before Alison's wedding, 1986.

I am writing this as both a daughter and a sister. This image of my sister and I with an old photograph of our mother, Norma, is very special to me. One of the gifts my mother gave us was a love for dance and movement. Everytime I look at this photograph, I see rhythm and movement, and thank her for that special, joyful part of her that she passed onto us. But I also see sadness and resignation on our faces, and wonder if we show these faces to the world often.

My mother died in January 1972, several months before her 43rd birthday. She had chronic breast problems throughout her life, and was in various stages of recovery and relapse during my high school years. I am pictured here in my karate uniform (gi) executing a technique. I began my training shortly after my mother's death in 1972; it was the only way I found to work through my anger, and grieve. I was 19 years old at the time of her death—at a crucial point in my own life—and full of guilt, sadness and sexual confusion. I always felt that I failed as a daughter and that my mother's disappointment in her family led to her breast cancer, and losing her will to live. In many ways, I tried to be my mother's mother.

My family role has been caretaker, and my sister was the family actress—very dramatic and demanded a lot of attention. My role was to "make nice." At an early age I learned how to avoid criticism, ridicule and punishment by being small and invisible. I admired my sister's courage in rebelling against my parents, but I felt manipulated and abused by the dynamics between my mother and sister. Often their battles put me in the "no-win" situation of trying to please two equally unreasonable and un-yielding parties—neither one interested in what I thought or how the family environment was affecting me. My mother really never knew what I felt or thought; she saw what she needed me to be. In my mother's Puerto Rican eyes, there were only two types of women; whores and madonnas. Reina's behavior cast her in the role of family whore; I was left with a rigid role of saintly behavior. I tried to meet her expectations, but in the end I felt so much resentment for not being accepted for who I was, and a loss of self-respect for living a lie. After 15 years, I still feel that pull of conflicting emotions that I felt during her illness—guilt, sadness, anger, despair.

I envy women who have had the opportunity as adults to come to terms with their relationships with their mothers. My mother always said she wanted to become frineds with her daughters, the way she had been with her mother. But I think she couldn't bear to look too closely at her own life and the compromises she had made, and resented Reina and me for having different ideas and attitudes. I still forget sometimes that she won't be back; we won't have another chance to be open and real with each other.

Valeria Ramirez

As I've gotten older and become a mother myself, I reflect on my mother in a different light than I did at the time she died. I was only 21, confused, and felt very guilty about her death. My mother and I had a very intense relationship. She saw much of herself in me, and that led to bitter clashes. My way of rebelling was sometimes quite self-destructive. Emotionally, I think we share many similarities; I see them more the older I get— both the negative and the positive.

My mother's generation married young and accepted a lot more than I have. Beneath her frustrations with her life was a talented, spirited woman. She wanted more for me and was afraid of seeing me become trapped in a life without options. Although I disagreed fiercely with her about the direction of my life, I think her basic value system was sound.

I have dreams for my daughter. I hope I will keep them in perspective with her growing independence. I hope, most of all, that she will love herself and find friends and a vocation that will give her life meaning. Perhaps that's all my mother ever really wanted for me. If she were alive, I wish I could share with her my feelings about being the mother of a daughter today. I believe that somewhere my mother can see that I am happy . . . I regret that we couldn't make our peace while she was alive. I also wish she could have known her granddaughter. For me, my daughter is not only a continuance of myself, but of my sister, mother, and grandmother. In her face I see a reflection of us all.

Reina Pickford-Ramirez

Reina Pickford-Ramirez, 32, hair-dresser, and Valeria I. P. Ramirez, 31, self-employed book-keeper, 1983. Their mother died in 1972.

Gertrude Garrison,
47, direct sales;
Amber Turnage, 22,
clerical worker, and
her baby, Jennifer
Turnage, three
months old, 1983.

Frances Rocha
Sheykhzadeh, 55,
management ana-
lyst, and Guilan
Sheykhzadeh, 22,
creative writing
student, 1987.

I have hope that my daughter Christine continues to realize her power and self-worth; that she always maintains balance with her energies and reaches her goals in harmony from within. I also hope she never relinquishes her ideals and falls prey to the pitfalls of our ever-changing society.

I feel good about Christine's happy zest for life, her confident ability to face challenges and overcome obstacles. She has a vital and enthusiastic approach to life that is infused with self-confidence. I think self-worth and independent motivation are at the vortex of her successes.

As a divorced, working parent of four, I was not always able to share as much time with Christine as I would have liked, but our times together were always meaningful and fun. Most parents of my generation were well versed in the teachings of Benjamin Spock. My guide was Dr. Haim Ginott's *Between Parent and Child.* Through the wisdom of that small book, early Montessori education, and my innate nurturing, I have a wonderful friend, my daughter Christine.

Fleta Sharpe

Ever since I can remember, I've loved mom because she has always recognized me as an individual in addition to loving me as a daughter. Thus, I've always felt unique and wasn't categorized as a daughter, a kid or a teen—I got to be all of those things in addition to being a daughter, corny as it may sound. I think early on mom realized that she didn't just have kids; what she had, though they were running around in diapers, were little people.

Growing up in a single-parent home was difficult at times, but mom always managed to keep smiling and encouraging. Even while working two jobs, she found the time to sit through hours of "singing," dancing to top-ten hits, and puppet shows with stuffed animals. I always wondered why mom never dated; she was attractive, nice, easy to talk to . . . It occurred to me later on that she thought being with the kids was more important than hanging out with the opposite sex for a boring evening of dinner, dancing, movies, candlelight-filled evenings, walks, intelligent adult conversation, excursions to romantic getaways.

Of course, the above mentioned tribute is not the whole story about my relationship with mom. Fire and brimstone aptly describe the mood of the terrible teen years. How many times she swore to send me to my dad's house if I was impertinent "one more time," I can't remember! Personally, I thought she was the demon of life! We fought over everything from what I should wear to how the state of my bedroom reflected the absolutely horrendous, chaotic state of my generation as well as mirroring

my personality. I remember wishing that I was old enough to live my own life without having to hear the tyrannical ragings of . . . a mother! The fights never lasted too long, even though I was considered the world's greatest sulker. Sooner or later things always got back on the right track and we were laughing and joking about one thing or another.

Sometimes I feel that mom is more like a sister. Our relationship is not bogged down in the patronizing, maternal "mother knows best" stereotype. Both of us feel that it's perfectly fine to be as open with each other as possible. Sometimes I think she's way out of line and vice versa, but that never matters because we respect each other's opinions. When we get together our conversations run the gamut of serious and intense to Abbott and Costello imitations. Most of the time we spend together is enjoyable. Both of us have a natural penchant to laugh at life rather than wallow in misery. From mom I received the gift of looking at life in the most positive way possible. Whether it means accepting things that can't be changed or doing one's best to keep things going, it's better with a smile. I feel closer to her than when we lived in the same house. (Possibly, because she no longer has to look at my unmade bed!) My mother is the most vital person I know.

Christine Sharpe

I thought of expressing how heartbreaking it is to be asked questions in the present tense about my mother; I wanted to elaborate on the sensation of longing I get whenever I look at the picture that Raisa took of my mother, my sister, and myself. Some day I will write pages on who Elissa Melamed was as a person, as my mother; but right now, all this touches a place in me that is much too raw. If there are words for such things, I haven't found them yet. Instead, I will endeavor to write about a spring afternoon that she and I spent together four years ago.

My mom was very open to learning new things, and throughout much of my adolescence I remember her running off to meetings, groups, and lectures. She'd ask one of us kids if we wanted to go with her to these events, and I, especially during my rebellious teens, scorned her for being too weird, and the gatherings for being too boring to bother with. One of the first indications of my own growth was when I started to accompany her on her various outings. I was just out of my junior year of college when one day I agreed to go with her to a talk about the Female Spirit in Judaism. I can remember the way that we acted out the ritual that was such a part of our lives whenever we were together. My mother dressed herself in bright colors and make-up, over consciously; she passed by the mirror several times, often posing right in front of it to scrutinize her expression, her stance, her presentation. I, more anxiously, echoed her movements, hoping that she'd approve of my weight, my clothing, and my hair. When she beamed at me, and remarked on how lovely my purple earring looked as it dangled close to my cheek, I felt exhilarated at the prospect of the afternoon we would spend together.

This sensation lasted all day. If I force myself, I can almost re-experience the way that the two of us sat on chairs outside, the sun so hot overhead that my mom put her shawl over her hair. I hear her eloquent questions to the speaker, and the way her voice sounded, high and slightly off-key, as she sang with the other women in the group. I see her hands holding the program of events or reaching over to hold mine quickly . . . I feel how soft they were . . . and I recall the way the gladness filled me that we were sitting there; the sun, the songs, the women, and the way that during this time I got to be completely her daughter. Our shared delight in the connection between us was sometimes powerful enough to transcend our growth in directions away from each other. There was a way in which our companionship sustained itself even as I made my adult life, and she continued with hers.

So it wasn't surprising that after the talk ended, a woman came up to us and began her sentence with, "Excuse me, I couldn't help but notice that you are mother and daughter." Oh, dangerous joy! People used to often tell us that we looked like each other. My mother would say that she felt complimented by it;

but for me, it was both a pride and a burden, for I thought she was beautiful. When we were asked to pose for a photograph, it seemed like an affirmation and an extension of the bond between us. It was a tangible way of expressing it to others; of seeing it captured on film for ourselves. My mother turned to me and said, "I'd like it if in the photos you look just as you do now, with that purple earring shining, just so, in your hair."

Today when I wear that earring, as when I look at the pictures that followed from that photography session, I inevitably think of that time with my mother. Not a day passes when I don't wish I could talk to her about my life since she died, to ask her things I still don't know the answers to. Yet some things I know she felt without her ever having told me. I'll bet that if I asked her now, she'd remember the smile that passed between us when a complete stranger recognized the way that we were related.

Mora Rothenberg

Elissa Melamed, 52, author, therapist, and peace activist; Mora Rothenberg, 22, graduate student; and Reina Rothenberg, 18, college student, 1983. Elissa Melamed died in 1985.

Gwen Liebl, 52, reg-
istered nurse practi-
tioner, and Susan
Liebl, 30, realtor,
1987.

Indu Mati Paul, 58,
homemaker, and
Ashima Roy, 38,
architectural drafts-
person, 1987.

Marylou Fitz-Murphy, 53, health care services, and her three daughters; Lisa Murphy, 33, hairstylist, shop owner (right); Maryellen Murphy, 23, artist; and Buffy Murphy, 31, travel consultant (left), 1983.

Billye B. Ericksen, 47, president and chief executive officer of her own electronic components firm, and Katherine Ericksen, 29, vice president of operations, 1983.

As I write this I look upon my daughter's photograph and catch a glimpse of what I call, "that look," a certain tilt of her head, the tension in her jaw, and I wonder if it is anger. Is it anger at me? I wonder if she, too, will yearn for a "mother," as I yearned for one, especially during her infancy and toddler years when I felt trapped and vulnerable. In my ignorance of the something called motherhood, I blamed my own mother who had failed to tell me or show me how to do it. I wonder if my daughter will ever wish she had received more of the "stuff" that mothers are traditionally known for. I wonder if she will become angered at the fact that the magic mother, the fantasy one, the one that is the alpha, the omega, the ultimate mother, was not the one who gave her life and sustenance. I wonder how long it will take her to come to those feelings as I, too, have finally come to realize that my mother just did not have "it." She did not have it because she, too, was not given the "it." Whether the "it" is a myth or reality, if one feels that there wasn't enough of it, then the feelings "are-feelings-just-the-same." Perhaps this missing "it" is in the nature of all human beings.

Tonight I recall one significant memory as I write this: There was a time I was on a pedestal. I observed it in my daughter's eyes as she looked up at me, as she accepted my values, as she comprehended our silent understandings. But one day, and I remember it clearly, though the date and time of year escape me, I witnessed in her vividly blue eyes my fall from grace. The betrayal had occurred, though to this day I do not know what event precipitated it. I did know, however, that from that day forward we would begin our conflict, which has been the conscious theme of our relationship since that time. However, it belies the fact we have a fierce love-friendship underneath this surface interaction.

Whatever legacy she admits to receiving from me, my daughter has formed her own powerful personhood. She radiates a joy of life, she is trustworthy, grounded in her own sense of purpose and self, and with tenacity reaches towards her own goals. They are not my goals. Outwardly, they do not resemble my goals except that the ingredients have come from the fact that she and I have never resembled a "normal" family. We have had to be creative together to find a level of interaction with the rest of the world. And from those building blocks, she has learned to create and fashion a lifestyle, a presence that is successful.

My daughter has been my teacher. From the early years, she has taught me about my process. She has been my mirror. She has unwittingly provided me with tolerance, patience, acceptance, and perseverance. She has provided me with humor, reminders of my spiritual existence, and most of all, she taught me to walk in balance. She is unaware of my struggle, however, as I was unaware of my own mother's. Until the day when she,

too, will walk the path of motherhood, she will not know, as I did not know, what those footsteps represent. And there is no one to explain it or describe it to her. Though our mothers try to prepare us, though psychologists and other professionals assume it is in our "natures" as women to be mothers, I state firmly that it is not true. Motherhood did not come naturally or easily for me, as it did not for my mother. I have lived these 22 years of my daughter's life wondering if I was the only woman, the only mother with these doubts or these understandings, for the true information seemed always to be a big secret. Now, even though I have met hundreds of other women who admit that mothering is not magical and is not just instinctual, I find that I still am surprised and relieved to hear it from others.

Mothers and their relationships with their daughters are enigmatic representations of what women do not wish to repeat in themselves. I have spent much of my life trying not to be like my mother. I have expended a lot of energy ignoring those parts of myself that reminded me of my mother. And yet, lo and behold, I discover that like the creature of the sea who continuously regrows its appendage every time it is severed from its body, I continually discover that my mother's behaviors appear in me, over and over and over again.

Given the level of information I had at the time, I did the best I could. Today, I am beginning to understand that the same thing was also true of my own mother. In that way, I am coming to learn how to forgive her. Only until I can fully forgive her, can I forgive myself. Today, my daughter challenges my entire notion of self. As I see my mother in me, I also see parts of my daughter that remind me of myself. Now, at this stage of my life it really doesn't matter whether she resembles some of my characteristics or behaviors, though I must admit that at one time I grieved at the fact that she had taken on some of my negative issues.

When I see that there are parts of me in my daughter which distress me, I have learned to stand back far enough, letting go of the outcome of her life, to focus on the fact that she is herself. And that she is just fine. In fact, she is quite a wonderful young woman. I am pleased to know her. Sometimes I can take credit. At other times, I know too that she is the one who has formed her own life, for I have only been the catalyst from which she was, is, and always will be in outward movement, spiraling ever outward away from me.

Nyla Gladden

Nyla Gladden, 43, writer and social worker, and Karina Assiter, 22, computer programmer and student, 1987.

Paula was born when I was 26 years old. She is my second child and also my baby. But she was a "toughy" compared to her brother. She really gave me a run for it. I mean it . . . I ran plenty, but I was young enough to have been able to handle her. She was a handful, and truthfully, she kept me on my toes.

Remembering back now, after so many years, I can honestly say I enjoyed all of it. I grew with her because there was so much to learn while raising her. I had to have answers to her questions (I used the dictionary and encyclopedia); and with her wit I had to keep pace with her. Even as a small child, Paula was vivacious and commanded attention, as she still does today. A mother has to be a parent, psychologist, friend, and objective observer, among other things. My darling Paula was, and is, still one of the greatest challenges and joys of my life.

I am very proud of my daughter, for so many reasons. The first is that she is *my* daughter. This may sound selfish, but I do share her with others, most definitely and especially with her husband. But at the same time, I do glory in the fact that she is mine and a part of me. Aside from being a daughter, she is also a good friend and lots of fun. I love to dance and have taught her every dance step I know. She is my favorite and best dance partner. She does the greatest charleston and jitterbug. She is also well-versed in her Jewish religion and in the values of Orthodox Judaism. I believe she keeps her faith because she knows who she is, where she comes from (her roots and Jewish history), and is comfortable with the tenets of Judaism. These feelings, in turn, bring us even closer in our mother-daughter relationship. Raising Paula has certainly taught me to live life to the fullest!

My greatest hope for my daughter is that she be happy and healthy in her life with her husband and future family. If she leads her life decently, (which she does and I am sure will continue to do so) she should have no regrets about her life. I have always told her there is no turning back, and that she should forge ahead to the future. I have confidence and trust in her to always come out on top. One of the important aspects of our relationship is the mutual trust, confidence, and love that we have for each other. Without these, I personally do not think that we could have had such a wonderful relationship.

The only advice I would give my daughter when her time comes to become a mother is: "Give love, have patience, be trusting, and raise your children together with your husband, not with surrogates."

Rae Guttman

To know my mother, Rae Guttman, is to know a truly multi-talented woman. She is creative, innovative, resourceful, and can do just about anything. My mother is a "take charge" person; she is a wonderful organizer and a very responsible individual. She has a sharp mind, and a keen ability to think ahead, to solve problems, and to consider every possible outcome of a situation before making a decision. My mother is extremely aware and "street smart"—two important qualities in dealing with today's society.

These inherent aspects of my mother's personality have become inherent aspects of my personality. I believe that the development of my personality is a direct result of my observing and learning from her over the years. I am quite fortunate to have a mother with such talents to learn from. I see our relationship as having two facets: one is the mother-daughter relationship, and no matter how old I get, my mother will always be "mommy" to me and I will be her youngest child. The other facet is our relationship as friends—my mother is my best friend, aside from my husband. She is young, vibrant, and fun to be around. I know that she is always there when I need her, and that I can always depend on her. I am also proud of my mother's accomplishments. Not only did she perform her "motherly duties," but she went to school to complete her college degree, and a Master's degree, while my brother and I were growing up.

One important aspect of my life that I thank both of my parents for is my Jewish upbringing and identity. We are Orthodox Jews, adhering to the timeless Jewish traditions. I am glad they gave me the opportunity to know my family's and people's history, and that I will be able to pass the traditions on to my children, and continue the chain.

Paula T. Guttman

Vicki and I have had what I will call an interesting relationship over the years. She is my firstborn, and as such, has always played a very important part in my life. My love for her has been deep and lasting, and has caused much joy as well as terrible pain, I believe, for both of us.

Being a young mother, and coming from a very tight-knit family that stressed excellence in everything attempted, I was fully prepared to shape my young daughter into exactly what I wanted her to be. Well, she surprised me. She decided to be what *she* wanted *herself* to be. I was stubborn—she was even more stubborn—and there were plenty of personality clashes and differences of opinion. She began at a very early age to teach me that Mother is *not* always right. And indeed, she wasn't.

I would have, if I'd have had the right to do so, steered Vicki in a very different direction from the one she chose. But this was not my life to live, but hers. She has done extremely well in the field she chose, and I am very, very proud of her talent and determination.

We have remained relatively close over the years, although she is away much of the time and the separations are sometimes quite long. There are still differences of opinion, and still, rarely, personality clashes—but always, always, always, there is the love.

Sylvia Brown

There are so many things I want to say about my mother and our relationship, which I feel is stronger now than it has ever been, although we see so little of each other. My mother taught me that being different was okay. She has braved two interracial marriages and lived as a divorcee supporting five children under the age of ten years. She also challenged the Catholic Church to marry again after her divorce—always ready to fight for her beliefs.

When I was a kid hanging around next to my mother in the store, people would walk up to me confused and ask if I was lost because they couldn't find the black woman anywhere. I was very polite and explained that, no, she's right here. My mother thought it was funny, but later on I realized that it really bothered me that people never could, by sight, connect me with my mother. We really came from such radically different backgrounds. She was raised a conservative Catholic in the Midwest with a strict "right and wrong" view of the world. For me though, with a white mother and a black father, it seemed that just being alive was breaking somebody's rules, and I never really felt as though I belonged anywhere. My mother tried her best to give me an education, and the broadest possible range of

experiences, but she left out an important key—integration with my black heritage and culture. I was ashamed of being black because all of the awakenings I had to the fact were rude and frightening; being called "nigger," chased home from school, spit at, pushed down, and beat up. Then I began to grow angry that I'd never been given an opportunity to learn about, respect, and feel proud of my black "half." The turning point came when I was 14, and in defiance of my mother's wishes, I grew my hair into an Afro. I knew she wanted to make it possible for me to get a head start in a world that was going to try and hold me back because of the color of my skin. But I also began to realize that denying myself is the greatest hindrance of all.

Our relationship has been rocky much of the time. I always seemed to want to do or be something she didn't approve of. I thought I was being original. Not until recently have I seen how well my mother taught me to be daring, experimental, and non-traditional, although I'm sure that often as not she's regretted it. I've been a very good student—repeating in many ways the same battles with my mom that she had with her own mother. My mother and I have spent literally years not speaking to each other, and in my self-righteous assertions of my own values, I often forgot to try and accept hers. Two years after this photograph was taken, my mother was hospitalized with breast cancer. I learned so much about her in that short week of operations; fear, mourning, vulnerability, and the joy of discovering the cancer had been arrested. We laughed and cried with each other and she said, "I had to wait until my mother was 70 to do this. I'm glad we didn't have to wait that long." Slowly, over the past few years, my mother and I fleshed out into people with each other, more than the two-dimensional mother/daughter act; but real women who share with one another our lives, loves and losses, sadness and joy.

Vicki Randle

Sylvia Brown, 52, typesetter, and Vicki Randle, 30, singer and musician, 1985.

Lucille H. Mendel,
66, patron of the
arts, and Jules
Mendel, 34, travel
agent, 1987.

Louisa Hoffmann, 66, patron of the arts; Patricia Strauss Gray, 35, dance teacher and choreographer; and Victoria Strauss Cummings, 31, commercial property manager, 1987.

For my daughter June, I hope she has emotional and spiritual fulfillment and success in her projects. She's talented and works hard, and has dreams. The one thing I'm afraid of for her is that, due to circumstances beyond her control, her projects and dreams will not be completed soon enough. I want her creative talents unhampered by financial troubles.

I'm proud of June's obvious creative abilities, her persistence balanced by a warm, affectionate, generous nature—demonstrative and childlike. Sometimes, she seems too driven and uncompromising about some things, almost a one-track mind. At this point, I do not presume to give her any advice, except perhaps to be less driven on some things. My regret is that she did not have more positive memories of her late father who was a complex and gifted person.

I think I was able to make June realize the importance of nurturing her spiritual side. For me, being a mother has made me flexible and unselfish.

Yolanda Millington

My mother's life in the Philippines was so different! Her studies were interrupted by the war and Japanese occupation, and she grew up in a rigidly Catholic society—matrilocal in the Chinese tradition—where the man's word was law and options for women were limited. Her postwar marriage to my dad was exciting, and was the social event of the season. In a way, it was a break from tradition as she was marrying a white man—one of the conquering knights in shining armor. But it was a difficult marriage, and as the eldest child, I absorbed their pain, frustration, and cultural misunderstandings, which filled me with despair. I wanted everything to be "right," and I wanted my mother to be happy. It seemed to me that after about age eight, she wore a mask of perpetual suffering. I never really saw who she was until after my dad died and she came into her own, blossoming in her own "now-free-to-manifest" strength. I admire her for that . . . for making the metamorphosis way after her spirit was seemingly crushed, and finally standing in her own light.

The most positive influence my mother has had on my life was to allow me the intrinsic freedom to follow my heart. I began to play music professionally before the wave of women's lib was even a crest on the horizon. There were no role models for a brown (Filipine-American) girl like me in any professional field, much less electric guitar! But when my sister Jean and I wanted to start a band in the 1960's, and my father strongly disapproved, my mother went behind his back to co-sign a loan for us at a music store. She could tell it made us happy . . . that the music itself made our hearts sing. She did not deny us any possibilities, however unconventional or beyond the range of her cultural references. The absence of any discouraging words was a major source of support in itself, and although we were playing air force bases and frat parties while barely 17 and 18 years old, she never doubted our conduct. She knew that this was our life's blood.

It's difficult to talk about what makes me angry about my mother. One has to separate the core of light and goodness from those behavioral characteristics that have to do with the mechanics of survival. In her case, as I believe with most women of her generation, my mother adopted passivity as a way of coping with both her father's, and then my father's, domination. It paralyzed her, and made her dysfunctional in relating to the world in an open, confident manner. I couldn't wait to leave that darkness, and rock 'n' roll provided the perfect opportunity. I must have been furious, but I didn't admit it to myself back then. How could I? I had numbed myself beautifully as best I could. We were all in a collusion of silence.

On the other hand, my mother seems to genuinely care about other people in a way I've had to learn. But that was part of my defense, and while I was numb to my feelings, it was hard to acknowledge that other people had feelings too. It was in my 20s that I finally began the unraveling, partly because of a spiritual quest that music could not help but lead me to. One door led to another and I've really changed.

Witnessing the transformations in each other has been a special part of our relationship. I could never have conceived of it just a short 20 years ago. We haven't lived in the same city since I left home at 19, and I've been on the road a lot . . . but still, the parallels are there. Spiritually and emotionally we're both seekers and are open to change. This is a great gift, and having the unique opportunity to watch the dramatic changes in each other —in just this lifetime—is a special blessing. I believe it is part of being born into this era of change as we near the 21st century. We've broken through so much pain and sadness, so much that held us back; I never thought we'd come this far. It's pretty unbelievable.

June Millington

Yolanda Millington, 63, business-woman, and June Millington, 34, guitarist and singer/songwriter, 1984.

As I sit to write about my relationship with my mother, my mind and heart are flooded. Not unlike standing at the banks of a swiftly flowing river that has to be forded, I don't know where to jump in.

It has been 13 years since my mother's death at the age of 59 from complications of breast cancer. Despite her physical absence, our relationship manifests itself continually in my life; in learned mannerisms, ongoing love for a mutual family, and in ever more prominent role conflicts in want of resolution. I am literally "of her" yet I am amazed that at age 36 I continue the task of individuating, separating, "birthing" the Karen Brummel who is unique, but inexorably connected to her. Sometimes I wonder how daughters ever do it.

At the time of her death, she did not know that I was to become a doctor. No doubt she realized I was smart, loving, and had a mind of my own. In this I am not unlike her. Yet her options were limited. While she encouraged me and took pride in my college education, I am quite certain that she never considered medicine as a career choice for me. Not that she would have thought it too difficult or beyond my grasp; it simply would not have occurred to her that I might try. Clearly, it occurred to neither of us at that time.

My mother, a bookkeeper until she was married in 1943, subsequently never worked for a wage outside her home. But work she did. Following three unsuccessful pregnancies, she was told by her doctor that she would never bear a living child. Yet at the age of 33, she gave birth to my eldest brother, the first of her five children. While my father worked long hours fitting fire sprinklers in construction sites, my mother worked to build a home of warmth, emotional and physical nurturance, and acceptance. We grew up with the security of her immutable love. It was my mother's spirit which spawned the openness and friendship reliably found in our family's home.

From my mother I learned the power of feeling. My fondest memories are of her tears. She cried unabashedly, in joy or sadness, whenever she felt the need. Despite my father's occasional ridicule or the perceived embarrassment of a guest in our home, she seemed to have no internalized shame in being a woman who displayed feeling publicly. I learned early from her example how not to dam the river of my own emotions. (Funny that one should have to learn that.) I grew up comfortable with expressing the depth of my feelings, my moods. At times I sensed that she felt I had learned this lesson too well. My feelings were not always pretty; "temperamental" she used to call me. I remember feeling hurt that the range of emotion I had learned to show was at times judged harshly by the very one who modeled the same for me. Though as the years have passed, I realize that it was often the darker emotions of anger,

anguish, or fear which seemed harder for her to accept in herself, which subsequently she found difficult to accept in me.

Like me, my mother lost her own mother to breast cancer. She must have borne what I call "unspeakable fear" of her own death from the same disease. Indeed, she never spoke directly of the fear to me, nor did I share my fears with her. Looking back, I see us each struggling with our own denial, each afraid of frightening the other. Realizing that we did the best we could at the time, my heart still longs for the missed opportunity to talk with her about these feelings. It has taken me many years to begin to grapple with my own fear of cancer. I have made a big dent in my denial by getting regular mammograms and talking openly with my husband, friends and family about these fears. I feel strongly that in so doing, I am freeing myself from being a victim of the disease that took my mother and grandmother at an early age. I plan to live a long life.

My memory of my mother's illness grows more vague with time. I recall the trips in and out of the hospital, the chemotherapy, the radiation, the suffering. Throughout, there was a healthy dose of denial about the progression of her disease. Yet despite pain and growing weakness, she remained hopeful. This was most poignantly evidenced to me by her purchase of several accounting books just weeks before her death. She told me of her hope to return to school, and perhaps to the work she loved when she was young. These plans were never realized.

On the morning of the day she died I sat at her bedside. Anticipating the wedding of my sister in three weeks, she had begun embroidering a square for the wedding quilt. Too weak to continue, I undertook the task of its completion . . . "God is Love"; gold thread on turquoise, I stitched. As I sat she became more restless, in moments semi-delirious, speaking almost inaudibly . . . "end of the trouble . . . end of the trouble." From the back bedroom came the sound of my youngest sister coughing, coming down with a cold. In an instant my mother was lucid; she opened her eyes and spoke to me in a distinct and mothering tone . . . "Karen, who is that coughing?" Within four hours she was dead.

No doubt stirred by the impact of her illness and death, and ironically, perhaps freed in her passing to pursue a role disparate from hers, I decided to become a doctor. A long haul through which I have sorely missed her loving support. Yet as I sat for this photograph, seeing the arm of her wedding gown gently draped over my doctor's bag, time was transcended and I felt her love flow over me like water.

It is a love that death cannot confine.

Karen Brummel-Smith

Karen Brummel-Smith, 36, physician, with her mother's wedding dress, 1987. Her mother died in 1974.

I'm a mother of nine children, five girls and four boys. I raised them all by myself, except for one. I had my first baby when I was 19. I supported my kids by weaving; that was my only trade. I had no other experience in jobs, so I had to weave rugs.

Now, at the age of 46, I'm a grandmother. Just last year I had my first grandkids, who are twin girls. Being a grandmother makes me feel good about it. One of my granddaughters is mentally handicapped, and I take care of her. I thought I was too old to take care of another child, but I was wrong. Now that I'm a grandmother, I know what it feels like being a grandma. I love both my granddaughters, and my heart aches when my grandchild gets sick. She's gone through several surgeries already at the age of one year. She's a tough little girl. Our prayers are always with her.

Keeping my granddaughter under my care keeps me occupied all the time. I really enjoy being with her. There's a home health care nurse who comes to our house, she's been a lot of help, and I appreciate her help.

Grandma Rose

I'm a daughter of a wonderful mother. She's a very special part of my life. She has done so many wonderful things for me that I'm pleased with. She raised me with a lot of love, and I thank her every day of my life. Although she and I had some rough times, such as most mothers who get after their daughters when something is done wrong. Sometimes I wish I wasn't a daughter—I would get so upset when my mother would sometimes say, "You went to school and graduated for nothing." Sometimes I compare my life to my mother's. Her life was rough raising eight kids with a lot of heart . . . that's something . . . my life is so much different from hers.

What pleases me is that people like my mother's kindness. She likes to help people a lot, especially at ceremonies, and she'll take my sisters and me along to help. I would like to be a good rug weaver like her, that's what I want from her for myself. She's had a rough life, I give her credit for raising me with great love. I guess that's what mothers and daughters are all about.

Charlotte Willie

On February 10, 1986 at 5 a.m., I was in tears and pain. I was admitted to the obstetrics ward. The morning had finally come, although I wasn't due until mid-March. I couldn't give a natural birth, so I had to have a Caesarean. I never knew how much pain it was to go through surgery. After I was back in the recovery room, one of the nurses told me I had a set of twin girls. I went to see my two beautiful girls, Valerie and Veronica Lee.

When they were five days old the doctor told me Valerie might have an infection. They took her to another hospital, and found out she had spinal meningitis. The doctors did x-rays on her head, and found fluid in her head, and most of her brain got damaged from that fluid. She's slow at growth now, and she's got real tense muscles in her neck, but a physical therapist works with her once a week, and she's starting to lift her head now.

It's very hard to see the twins, one healthy and one with problems. I deal with it through prayer, and I feel a lot better when I talk to other parents whose kids have spinal meningitis. My other daughter, Veronica Lee, is really patient with Valerie. She knows it's her sister . . . she hugs her and kisses her . . . and she tries to get Valerie to play with her. I am a single parent, and my mom is now the legal guardian of Valerie because I don't have the transportation to take her to the hospital whenever she gets sick. I'm real glad that my mom was very kind to take her into her heart to care for her. I love both my daughters, and my mother. They're my first kids, and my mom's first grandkids.

For other parents who have sick children, just keep faith and keep praying . . . and just thank the Lord you have the child . . . and to love the child, and that way the child will get better.

Brenda Willie

Rose Willie, 46,
weaver, and her
daughters (left to
right); Charlotte
Willie, 20, beader,
Brenda Willie,
23, beader, and
Jennifer Willie, 12.
The twins, Valerie
and Veronica Lee,
1 year, are Brenda's
daughters, 1987.

I hope my daughter finds her heart's desire, and that she realizes her full potential with no obstacles (or few) in her path. Right now, I am especially proud of how far she's gotten in building her own business, and the respect and trust her clients have in her expertise. But I'm afraid sometimes of her getting hurt because she always over extends herself for others.

Looking back on being a mother, if I could do anything differently, I would be more structured—I was too laissez faire. I would have liked Joyce to have had piano lessons, and I would have taken her to plays, but my bad marriage stopped me from doing a lot of things with all my children. I passed on to my daughter my obsession with food, but on the good side, she also has my generosity, fierce loyalty, and she is a social animal, just to name a few.

I've always been a mother, it seems, although I had my first child when I was 20. I'm 52 years old now, and motherhood is my occupation and lifestyle. I feel very enriched. My children are my best friends. Although Joyce is of the "new age," she still wants the basic goodies from life—children and emotional ties—and I would do anything I could to help her achieve her dreams.

My advice to my daughter about being a mother is to be more directive than I was. To teach her children to be involved and creative and loving. To know, as my daughter knows, that I am always here for her, no matter what. But I trust Joyce, she'll know what to do when the time comes. That's another thing she got from me, good judgment.

Rose Goldman

Whatever capacity for kindness and compassion I have, comes from my mother. I don't always agree with her methods, but her survival instinct is strong, and from her I've learned how to use my brains to make it.

Unfortunately, my mother thinks she still has the right to exert a strong influence on my life, and her "fears" for my future are a major source of conflict.

My mother escaped the strong will of her mother by marrying my father. I escaped by leaving home at 18, but my mother has yet to acknowledge the space between us. However, I am hopeful that as my mother's fears are allayed—when I marry and have children—the gap will be bridged.

Joyce Ann Goldman

Rose Goldman,
50, paralegal,
and Joyce Ann
Goldman, 30,
entrepreneur, 1985.

Eva Liplewsky, 61,
retired business-
woman, and
Sophia L. Fuchs, 34,
foreign language
teacher, 1983.

Eva Tillery, 64, retired, and Linda Tillery, 36, singer/ songwriter, 1984.

Mi amorosa Anna. She was barely ten years old when she asked me if she could take physical care of my daughter Lupe who had muscular dystrophy. Lupe was hospitalized at the time, and her brother Raul had passed away some months before that. Every weekend, for three years, Anna would feed Lupe through an intravenous tube, and bathe her. I was astounded by Anna's strength . . . a child taking care of an older sister like that. She continued this responsibility until the day Lupe died. That day, Anna told me she must've loved Lupe too much because she didn't want to see her after the doctors told us she died. These were all the things that Anna had grown up with, things that were as much a part of her own identity as they were of Lupe's. How can I not admire her?

I am also very proud of my daughter Bea. As the oldest, she shouldered a lot of responsibility at a very early age. During my most difficult years, she was always my friend and understood my situation with kindness and without judging me. She listened to me when she was a teen during the 60s when I was frightened about all the unrest among the youth of this country. I admire her strength and spirit of struggle. She has been a good example for Anna. I also admire Bea for all that she has done in the community—she's a woman full of love for her family and everyone around her. I am sure that God helped me very much along the way. I always tried hard to communicate with my daughters, from the time they could speak, and especially during their teen years. Anna was a little more difficult, but she taught me many things. All the good and the bad that we've shared, it is a dream come true—after all that, to be able to see and enjoy my grandchildren, and to love them as best I can.

Guadalupe Olvera

My mom took care of two disabled children for 34 years, and was married to a man who degraded her and blamed her for all the misfortune in his life. Yet, she alone disciplined a family of six children who all grew up to be college graduates while on welfare. Her influence has been profound. Her sense of power over her destiny, and belief that God blessed her because her cross made her children stronger, has given me a positive outlook on my life. She was able to raise my brother and sister, who had muscular dystrophy, to be independent and reach for the moon. My brother Raul wanted to be a Hell's Angel, so my mom thanked God for his disability. My sister Lupe was on a respirator and could only move two fingers, yet she was sensitive and feminine. She had pen pals from six countries, published a play, and had a love affair because she didn't want to die a virgin! My brother and sister gave us an appreciation for life and death. My mom gave them total love, attention, and sacrificed her own ambitions and wants for her children.

The most difficult part of our relationship has been the way my mom treats her daughters as independent adults, and yet her sons, for whatever reason, she treats as dependent adults. She is there to guide their adult decisions, and this need to take care of her boys tends to give a false sense of stability. We constantly argue about this. However, I am most pleased with her love of politics and sense of power. Also, our ability to share our plans, and help each other through the difficult times, are important to me. She is there for my children, and teaches them about our Mexican culture. She shares our family stories so that her legacy will be known by my children and their children.

Beatriz Olvera-Stotzer

Throughout most of her adulthood, my mother lived an extraordinarily painful life. Somehow, she endured each tragedy and managed to shield me from growing up bitter and cynical. Very few people have this tremendous ability to leave pain behind in the face of adversity, and move forward without damaging the people they love. My mother mastered the delicate balance of resilience and fortitude with passionate and unconditional love and loyalty for her children.

The most difficult part of our relationship is when our points of view clash. On certain subjects, my mother is stubborn and convinced that her point of view is the gospel truth. I used to be angry, mostly in high school. My mother had a difficult time dealing with my burgeoning sexuality. Because of my hyperthyroid, I had developed physically when I was quite young. This made her nervous, and at the time, I thought rather paranoid. She tried to restrict my life in meaningless ways and I became rebellious. I had a difficult time accepting that she had always treated me like an adult in other aspects of my life, but my maturity was not taken into account when it came to men and dating. Consequently, I resorted to lying about the most normal adolescent activities, out of fear. The sad part about this is that I really wanted to be close to my mother and share my feelings, but her own fears kept me away.

It's funny how age can mellow one's outlook. I no longer feel anger toward my mother. She made some mistakes, but given her circumstances, I am certainly not one to judge. The thing that pleases me most about my mother is that she has forgiven herself for not being perfect. She has allowed herself the freedom to make mistakes and to love herself through indulgence in happiness and fulfillment after many years of surviving a tragic life. She finally sees that her children, for whom she struggled nearly 40 years, are leading productive and responsible lives.

Anna Olvera Cole

Cleofas Ríos, 84, homemaker and great-grandmother; Guadalupe Olvera, 62, homemaker and grandmother; Beatriz Arcelia Olvera-Stotzer, 36, legislative affairs representative, and Anna Olvera Cole, 27, graduate student in business, 1987.

This daughter, Miriam, is the oldest of three children. I had great hopes for her to have an improving influence on her fellow citizens. My fears for her were more physical than spiritual, and I was always very concerned about her physical fitness and health.

Miriam is a beautiful human being by appearance as well as thought. I am proud of her many-sided capabilities, intellectual as well as dexterity. She always seemed able to do anything. She is a born leader, but sometimes too bossy. She is a great friend to many—something I was lacking. I am disappointed that she has no children, she would have been a great mother.

I hope she will always know the importance of independence, and the value of intellect and beauty over material gains. My daughter has raised my consciousness as a woman, and she brings me great happiness. I'll never be alone.

Anne Frank

My mother, Anne Heymann Frank, is a very intelligent and sensitive woman who has endured a lot, and has taught me her endurance and strength of will. She has always believed in me—in my strength and intelligence—and she has always been candid in answer to my questions. We have had good times together visiting art museums, taking walks, working in the kitchen, talking over family stuff.

My life is radically different from hers. She grew up in Germany in comfortable circumstances; my early years were as a child of refugees, speaking two languages. Temperamentally, I'm intense, explosive; my mother has a lot more patience—a quiet, factual irony to my sanguine moods. She has been in a stable marriage for more than 40 years, and has three children. At 40, I am childless and single, and have moved around the country quite a lot.

I am pleased that in spite of our differences, she understands and often agrees with my ideals and commitments. She is a very tolerant woman and cares about me with a true comprehension of all the differences. I am also pleased that our relationship has come to this peaceful place; it wasn't always so.

Miriam Frank

Anne Frank, 70, retired registered nurse, and Miriam Frank, 35, labor educator, 1983.

Just two months before this photograph was taken my father had died, and this was my mother's first visit to my home even though I had lived here off and on for 16 years. The photograph captures many of the struggles my mother and I were having at the time: my father's recent death, and my mother coming face-to-face with my lesbianism and my friends. Moreover, both of us were feeling the vast distance between us . . . our lives, our choices, our styles. My mother is legally blind and deaf, and her world is very limited by these disabilities. I have perfect vision and hearing.

An important influence my mother had on my life was believing in me wholeheartedly. As a child growing up, she had a great sense of joy and fun. She had many friends and loved them all dearly, and was very physical with me, which was her clearest way of communicating.

The most difficult part of our relationship occurred when I was 16 and leaving home early because I was not getting along with my father at all. He was home all the time because he became disabled from emphysema when I was 14. My older sister was an incest survivor, and I grew up in the fear of "me next." My mother behaved in the typical fashion of "collusion." To this day, she refuses to believe my sister or discuss it with her. Leaving home as fast as I could broke my mom's heart in some ways. I was her "baby" and she wanted me at home until I finished high school. My survival was more important than her need at the time.

My anger towards my mother is related to her not protecting me as a child. Some of this could not be helped with her very limited vision and limited hearing. I remember a little bird once flying into our home when I was young and she fainted in fright . . . I had to cope with the bird. My deepest anger towards my mother today is her staunch refusal to talk to my sister. My mother asked me a few years ago, "Well, if it were true that dad was molesting your older sister, then why didn't she tell me?" I answered, "If you didn't believe her at age 43, why on earth would you have believed her at age seven or nine?" My mom then promised to talk to my sister, but in the four years since, she has never done so once.

A year ago, my mother chose to move to the same city where I live. My deepest regret was her decision to move away after only six months here. I had to accept this rejection. In that half of year I learned more about who my mother really is from the point of view of myself as a 40-year-old woman . . . a very different picture than childhood memories. Prior to this period, I saw my father as the patriarch, the authoritarian despot that victimized my family with his actions. However, his behavior was overt and readable by all. My mother on the other hand, is covert and manipulative in ways I never dreamed to be a part of her character. Her symbiotic relationship with my father started

making a lot more sense. She was stronger and less a victim than I thought the case. Many years ago a dear friend once said she thought the nuclear family was basically "incestuous and cannibalistic . . . that is to the extent that members of the family could not handle their incestuous feelings towards each other, they emotionally cannibilized the other family members." Certainly, my family was no exception to her statement.

My mother married my father to get away from her domineering mother. On the other hand, I left home to get away from her domineering husband. I lived in four different homes in high school before striking out on my own completely at 19. My life has always been about taking risks, being intellectually stimulated and creative in artistic ways. In contrast, my mother never could work out of the home, never had her own money, nor the infinite array of choices I have been blessed with. I have chosen lifestyles that ranged from beatnik, hippie, radical in my youth to feminist, lesbian, artist in my maturity.

One of the things I've always respected about my mother and my father was their commitment as communists in the 1930's and 1940's to build a better world for themselves, their children and their society. Their roots gave me the strength, courage and integrity to dare to be different. The other great thing my mother and father gave me was a sense of self-reliance. They were working class people who struggled their whole lives to give us a better life. We lived in trailers and moved all over Southern California during the McCarthy period while I was very young. I worked from an early age. They taught me to take pride in whatever work I did. The work ethic instilled so early has sustained me in creative and economic ways ever since.

Jan Marie Du Bois

Lois DuBois, 65, re-
tired, and Jan Marie
DuBois, 36, French
tapestry artist and
accountant, 1983.

The most positive thing my mother did for me was to show me that all people and all cultures deserve respect. She came from a bicultural family background and did not have tolerance for racism or religious bigotry. We lived in a bigoted, Biblebelt of Kansas, and although my mother wasn't a political activist, she was a vocal liberal in a stronghold of midwestern conservatism. Racist or religious slurs by children or adults were not allowed in her home, and children who used such putdowns, were reprimanded and sent home, and then she would call their parents.

My mother wrote a daily column for the "Wichita Eagle & Beacon," which was the leading paper in central Kansas. She was a member of the American Press Women's Association, and she was active in church groups and women's organizations. She never really spoke about "politics" per se, and wasn't affiliated with any of the political parties, but she was concerned about social issues through her writing. In her daily column, she profiled many outstanding women from different ethnic and religious backgrounds in the community.

I was very proud of my mother. She taught me that women can and must think for themselves, and that they will be respected for it. The negative side of our relationship stemmed from the fact that she really wasn't prepared for motherhood. I was the first of her three children, and was born in 1943 during World War II. My father was in the navy, and it was a very difficult time for her. She'd been an outstanding college student, but had dropped out to marry my father before he was sent overseas. In her search for independence, she'd become isolated from her own mother and family in rural Oklahoma.

I can't recall much about my mother during my early childhood, and I can't recall if I was physically abused at the time or just badly neglected due to her states of depression. What I remember is having a terrible fear of her. As difficult as it is for me to say, I was afraid of my mother. Part of me was always afraid of her, even until the time of her death.

She was incapable of showing me physical affection or giving me emotional support. She couldn't express love—except in her writing—and never spoke of personal problems or relationships. Her approval was conditional, and I was expected to be a super achiever academically and socially. The main things she tried to give me were her artistic skills and intellectual values. My personal life was of interest to her only insofar as it affected her ambitions for me. As a very young child, I realized that it was senseless to argue with my mother because of her irrational anger, and that I had to seek guidance from other people and trust my own judgement. For me to do what I needed to do, meant

incuring her wrath, and often her complete rejection. I accepted the irrational side of my mother from an early age, and went on with my life. As a young adult, there were times when we weren't on speaking terms and I wasn't allowed to come to her home. Those were difficult years for me, but I learned how to survive independently without her.

During my childhood, I had very close feelings for my maternal grandmother in Oklahoma who was the person who really gave me warmth and love. My grandmother was a Native American woman who had raised a large family on a small farm. Her life was about bringing up her family, gardening, canning, cooking, making clothes, and having intimate afternoon talks with relatives and close friends. I have many positive memories of the time I spent with her, and in a very real sense, my grandmother is the person I identify with as my mother to this day. She was affectionate, and at the same time, she expected me to carry out certain responsibitlities on the farm. As a young child, I worked alongside her picking potato bugs off the plants, killing chickens, and plucking the feathers that we used for making pillows.

The key to a lot of my mixed feelings about my experiences as a daughter are the conflicting memories I have of my mother's uncontrollable anger, compared to my grandmother's firm, but rational discipline, which was tempered by understanding and affection. The memories with my grandmother still sustain me during difficult times in my life. My grandmother's warmth and honesty have given me faith and trust in people, which has given me the ability to love.

Linda G. Wilson

Linda G. Wilson, 37, photographer and photography curator, with her mother's singing dress, 1981. Her mother died in 1979.

Adriana C. Vivanco,
wife and mother,
and Lydia Diaz de
Leon, ballerina,
1987.

Frosene Sonderling, 66, vice president of a radio company, and Maria Michaels, 44, consultant, 1987.

I am a survivor. I watched my mother suffer for years with cancer and finally die in December 1984. Another member of my family has been struck with cancer. My two daughters and I have been the victims of crime, and I have been divorced. Despite all our hardships in the last five years, we are doing well. I feel that my work has helped me better understand the traumas in my personal life. My divorce clients have given me many insights into the ways in which loss manifests itself. They also have the endless capacity for survival that human beings demonstrate when faced with serious personal problems and identity crises.

My father died when I was nine and my memory of him is fragmented. I was raised in a matriarchal household, my strongest attachments having been to my mother and grandmother, who were both single-parent heads of households. My mother was enormously influential in my self-concept as a woman. The past has been a constant reminder to me of the pitfalls and potential in being a woman. My mother was raised in a Victorian household and dominated by a father who had contradictory responses to the women in his life. I recently learned, for example, that my grandmother, who was a leader in the suffragette movement in Ohio, was not permitted to go outside in the daylight when she was pregnant because my grandfather considered the sight of a pregnant woman unseemly. Yet, my grandfather was known for his liberal and progressive political leadership. Despite the restrictions placed on women, in my mother's home scholarship was encouraged. My mother's intellectual aspirations were reflected by her attendance at Swarthmore. Like many women of her generation, she never fulfilled all her career ambitions; she had problems resolving the fact that she had not entered law as her father had. I think that in many ways I acted out the side of her personality which sought to prove itself in the professional world of her father. She was, I believe, both proud and jealous of my accomplishments. I, as a result, was given many mixed messages about my work.

On the other hand, my mother was very positive and clear in other respects. She had an incredible survival instinct, a lust for life, a love of the English language, history, and elevation of the human spirit through creative effort. It is interesting that my mother, whose mother died when she was only two weeks old, was able to convey to me an almost animal dedication and enthusiasm for parenting. I have also learned from the mistakes she made as a parent: I have learned that to be a woman is to nurture for the purpose of letting go. I hope that my daughters will have both families and careers. However, I hope they will value being a parent enough to realize that it is worth sacrificing some career advancement and monetary rewards in return for taking the time to be a mother. I hope that they will marry men who know how to nurture themselves as well as my daughters, and are willing to share in raising children as well as cooperate over the little issues necessary to make work possible for both of them.

Elizabeth L. Bennett

There are certain qualities I have always greatly admired about Mom. The quality of education she received as a child, and the enthusiasm for knowledge she retained, created in her a vast reservoir of information and spirit. She could contribute fresh insight to almost any conversation and make history and the arts come alive; not only for herself but for those around her.

A devout eccentric, mother dispensed quickly with superficialities when relating to people. Money, homes, clothing, pretense, were of little concern to her. A person's integrity and experiences were the important qualities. Obviously, not all of us are like that, or even want to be like that, but these qualities made her friendships particularly close and the loyalty of her friends very great.

We're all wearing "ruanas"—those blanket shawls on our shoulders—in the photograph. Ruanas were one of mother's wardrobe staples, along with Birkenstock shoes and solid-colored pants. To her, ruanas embodied the most practical in outerwear attire, mostly because they accommodated heavy fabrics and blousy sleeves, which she wore a great deal. To me, ruanas were another testament to her eccentricity, something I was always trying to minimalize. I've never seen my sister Libby wear one outside this photograph; Kathy still owns a few; and I keep the very fine, handwoven one mother gave me years ago boxed neatly under my bed. Like a recessed gene, ruanas are very much a part of the family, but have little to do with anyone of us daughters individually.

In retrospect, my mother's stamina to her convictions and the integrity behind her value system relfected, in part, the privilege and freedoms of financial independence. Regardless, I am very grateful to her for the example she set in these areas. Her interest in things outside herself, the vitality of her spirit, were a constant reminder of the joys to be had by extending the use of one's mind and one's heart.

Ardele Leavelle

Olwen Morgan, 59, actress, poet, and composer; Elizabeth Bennett, 36, lawyer; Kathy Leavelle, 35; Ardelle Leavelle, 27, 1983. Olwen Morgan died in 1984.

Margo changes my life in some way each time we are together; new awareness, new insights, new dimensions of her as a person, and renewed appreciation of her as a daughter. She is always generous in sharing her discoveries and new horizons with me. With Margo, life is a kaleidoscope. Having a controversial daughter like Margo is a challenge, and I like challenge. Perhaps that is one trait she inherited from me. From hatcheck girl in the Colony Club in Seattle to co-organizer of the International Congress for the Rights of Prostitutes in Amsterdam (yes, I was there); from a YWCA room to a 200-year-old elegantly renovated post office in Southern France (yes, I am there); from driving a tractor on her father's farm in a small Pacific Northwest community to riding into the San Francisco Cow Palace on an elephant to the accolades of 15,000 people attending her celebrated Hookers' Masquerade Ball (I was there, too); to me, these are a few of the progress markers that have punctuated my pride in her ability to achieve her goals.

If there are disappointments, it has nothing to do with her choice of crusade to which she has devoted almost 30 years of her life—the decriminalization of prostitution. Who else would have the courage? It does have something to do with the lack of recognition and credibility—and money—for the social changes she has effected. Years ago, at the beginning of Margo's crusade for the rights of prostitutes, people would ask me how it felt to be her mother (such gall!). In reply, they usually got an hour's lecture on her hard work, the rights of women, and the changes that were happening because of her work. It paid off. Now, they ask me what new thing she is doing. (That takes more than an hour.) The important thing to me is that now we can talk about the issue without embarrassment on anyone's part.

It's been said, "Once a mother, always a mother," or conversely, "Once a daughter, always a daughter." I find that sometimes, magically, that changes and suddenly you are woman/friend or the daughter becomes the mother and the mother becomes the daughter, depending on age and circumstances. I cherish the ever-changing emphasis and rely on its inevitability. Unfortunately, my daughter inherited my compassion for the underdog and a tendency to romanticize life and relationships. I live with fear, constantly, because of the craziness of the world and my daughter's vulnerability and visibility. It is only because of my faith in her talent as a "survivor," and knowing that she has a worldwide network of dedicated friends and family that I can sleep at night—with a little help from my own personal faith. As her mother, I need to feel that my unconditional support of her crusade provides a buffer for the frustrations and antagonisms she has suffered over the past 30 years. In this, she indulges me.

Dorothy St. James Wachter

My mother's unconditional love and support, her compassion, perception, and willingness to be there in time of need and celebration with emotional support, and sometimes with some desperately needed cash, has made her the most important figure in my life.

I suspect that my teenage rebellion years were difficult for her, but luckily, I grew out of it without putting too much of a strain on her love. Now, the only strain in our relationship is the distance separating us. Her choice of a second husband was a strain on both of us for a few years, but time has mellowed him. He, also has "grown out of it" and now is the loving and supportive person that she deserves . . . except that he's not as rich as I would wish for my mother's sake (and for mine, I suppose!). He has come to accept our personal differences and not blame my mother for them.

Our lifestyles have been totally different. Mom has lived in the traditional way (home and family) whereas I was the one who left a husband and child and lived a single, and rather promiscuous life up until the past few years. Now, I am in a committed relationship with a woman 11 years younger than myself. My political commitment has tended to shape my life into something very different from the other women in my family, but we share many of the same qualities. It seemed to be the men in the family whose energies and talents turned them into "black sheep." It was my mother who encouraged me to do whatever I thought was right for me.

My move to Europe was for the purpose of organizing internationally for hookers' rights, finding considerably more support for the idea in Holland than in the United States. American feminists had gotten sidetracked on the anti-porn idea, and the conservatives write me off as being "pro sex." The 1st World Whores Congress was hosted by the Dutch and resulted in the formation of the International Committee for Prostitutes' Rights, of which I am President.

I'm pleased with my ability to have lived for 50 years without overtly compromising my integrity (which may explain my lack of money and is something I may live to regret), but I hope that it doesn't put a damper on my independence and outspokenness, attitudes that I definitely learned from my mother. If I were to wish for some qualities of my mother's, they would be her graciousness and her generosity. However, I think that I perceive those qualities as bordering on self-effacement, which is something that I guard against and which may explain my defiant posture at times. I would hope that it wouldn't offend the ones I love, especially my mother, and I'm sure it doesn't.

Margo St. James

*Tema Fastman, 63,
retired school
teacher, and Raisa
Fastman, 34, pho-
tographer, 1983.*

Dorzella Estes, 67,
retired beautician;
Mary Watkins, 47,
composer, pianist
and songwriter;
and her daughter,
Sherron Dawkins,
23, 1987.

When my daughter Geraldine was born, I was thrilled. My first babies were twin boys, and I lost one shortly after birth. Then I had another boy, and I lost him in an automobile accident when he was three years old. It was very tragic. When my daughter was born she saved me—she brought me happiness once again. What I have always wanted for my daughter is that whatever she decides to do, she do it well. I have always told her that if something doesn't go right, just forget about it, and go on to the next thing. I told her, "Your name is Ferraro. In Italian it means iron. You can bend iron, but you can't break it." I always remind myself of that too. Nothing is final. If one thing fails, go on to the next. I lost my husband when I was 39. I was devastated, but I kept on working and living for my children.

My daughter is very protective of me. I've been sick, and she and her family are very good to me. I am grateful to them for that. The hardest part for me with my daughter was when she lost the election for vice president. It was terrible. I felt that if she had won, she would have been such an asset to our country. Her ideas are wonderful. In the beginning, it was very hard, but we know we have to move on. Being a mother, I have learned that you have to give a lot of yourself. Also, that you have to listen to your children; they are human beings—people—no matter how young they are. I have always talked to my children with respect, even when they were babies. And they always returned that respect. If my granddaughters decide to have children, my advice to them will be, "Love your baby, give it all the care it needs and more if possible, and give it every minute you can. Giving love gives happiness. Without happiness, there is nothing."

Antonetta Ferraro

There are two major influences that my mother has had on my life. First, she instilled in me a "can-do" attitude: You can *do* whatever you want, and you can *be* whatever you want. Second, my mother gave me the exact same educational opportunities that she gave my brother. She was very forward-looking—the 80s feminist in 1945. When I was growing up, in an ethnic Italian home little girls were usually not treated the same way as little boys . . . except in mine. When I was 16, and graduating from high school, I wanted to go to college. My uncle said to my mother, "Why bother, Antonetta, she's a girl. She's pretty, she'll get married." Well, my mother did bother, and thank God she did. I went to college.

My mother had a difficult childhood. She is very smart but she never received a formal education because her father had a stroke when she was quite young, and she had to work to help support three younger siblings. My mother missed not having a formal education and that's why it was so important to her that both of her children go to college. My father died when I was

eight, and my mother had to raise her two children alone. The Social Security System was young and there were no benefits to help her. Day care did not exist. My mother had to go to work to support us so she sent me off to boarding school. She did without a lot of things in order to provide for us, much like other single heads of household in this country today. Her experience is undoubtedly the reason that I have great empathy for working women. The most difficult part of my relationship with my mother is watching her age. She was, still is, a beautiful woman. But she used to be very vibrant. Now she has osteoporosis which makes her seem even more frail. I wish my mom would focus more on herself and not worry about me. But as she grows older, I realize that she doesn't know how much longer she has, so she holds on to every minute, and that's fine.

As a mother, my biggest regret is that I was too hard on my oldest child, Donna. I was too much. I wanted her to be perfect. At four years of age, Donna was taking violin, tap dancing, and swimming lessons. She was reading and doing math problems. I pushed too hard, and for 25 years, I've felt guilty about it. I was easier on my other two children. (And the dog is a disaster . . . she runs our lives!) If I could do it over, I'd let Donna be two years old at two, and not worry about perfection. I am pleased that my children have developed a deep sense of security—independence, yet interdependence on one another. I love watching Donna and Laura together. I never had a sister. I evidently missed something special. They live in a home where we deal with problems together, and never take our frustrations out on each other, no matter what goes on in the world around us. I hope, if they marry, that they become a family where they get strength from each other as they have gotten strength from us. To cope with life's challenges, and then turn around and say, "That's behind me, now let me get on with the rest of my life."

Geraldine A. Ferraro

Figuring out who I am, as opposed to being my parents' daughter, has been an issue for me in the past few years. A lot of the time I'm juggling between obligations to myself, and obligations to my family. It's probably a little bit harder for me because when my mother ran for vice president I was 18. I still had a lot of growing to do. What I derive the most joy from is that I have always been proud of my mother. She has never embarrassed me. I want my mother's energy. She doesn't seem to get tired of any endeavor she takes up, be it family or career or Christmas dinner. That's something I completely take for granted. I don't aspire to be exactly like my mother; probably the same values, but different interests and priorities. What I want more of for myself is the sense of being a free spirit and being spontaneous. I also want more privacy.

Laura Zaccaro

Antonetta Ferraro, 82, retired; Geraldine A. Ferraro, 51, attorney and author; and Laura Zaccaro, 21, student, 1987.

My mother came to the United States at the age of 17, marrying a man twice her age, and facing prejudice and cultural shock, including being put in a concentration camp in the U.S. during World War II. Mother tried to raise me in a typical Japanese way, always telling me what to do and what she wanted me to be as a grownup, forever lecturing on filial piety, duty, obligation, and gratitude. I regret I didn't pay more attention when she was talking about her family and background . . . the give and take without the strain between mother and daughter. There are many questions I would like to ask her about her life before she was married, growing up in the Meiji era, just after Japan stepped into modern times.

I was not happy with how she badmouthed my father. Mother grew up in a samurai background, and raised as a "young lady" with all the refinements. Mother was a lot younger than Father, and he must've been set in his ways, leaving Japan in his early 20s. Mother felt she married beneath her . . . even though she was given a choice by her parents to turn him down, she married him to enable her to come to the U.S. I never had a decent talk with my father; he died when I was 15 and he was 62. My life was different from my mother's; I was born and raised in the U.S. Life was easier for the Nisei (second generation), with no language or cultural barriers. Mother worked hard, the driving force of the family, and did all she could to make life easier for her children. Like many Japanese mothers, she was self-sacrificing and a martyr when it came to her children. "Ga man" —to bear it—loses something in the translation. I was the youngest of three, spoiled by my mother, and rebellious. Nevertheless, I was the one she depended on and became her care-giver towards the end of her life. That didn't come about by choice, and I wasn't happy with the responsibility, but filial piety, duty, obligation, and a pinch of guilt came forth and I did the best I could. This way, I was able to show my gratitude for all she did for me.

As for my own mothering, I still have doubts as to my "laissez faire" upbringing of my children. Did I do the right thing? Perhaps there was something correct in my mother's way. I was so hellbent on doing everything the opposite, I probably went overboard in the other direction. Whatever doubts I have, I learned how difficult it is to be a mother. When I see my daughter doing some of the same things with her daughter that I did as a mother, I must've done something right.

Emiko Ota

I guess every mother wants her daughter to become the perfect woman that she failed to become, as awful as it sounds. My mom is caring, compassionate and a great believer in fair play. My daughter Nikki is exactly as I want her to be. She is creative and artistic.

Mom was a talented athlete, but never learned to swim because Japanese were not allowed in the public pools when she was young. Unlike many other Japanese-Americans, she never kept her war internment experience a secret from me, and even encouraged me to write a paper on it in high school as well as on other little known instances of racial injustices in this country. Her great love is basketball at any level, and she not only attended and drove kids to all her children's and grandchildren's games, but she was the rooter most likely to get a technical foul for cussing out the referees. I admire and love her for not being like everyone else's mom, and I hope my daughter feels the same about me.

My daughter is the warmest and friendliest kid I know. She is unbelievably accepting of people, and despite her being a rather typical teenager, we do not have horrendous confrontations and fights. I hope she realizes that she is at a wonderful time in her life, and that she believes her potential is limitless. I also hope that when she's my age she feels the same. We both get a kick out of people's reactions when they meet the two of us as mother and daughter, as does my mom when the two of them are out together. I hope she has the strengths to survive disappointments that may come her way, and know that she doesn't have to seek my approval—she's already got it, for keeps.

Leslie Lethridge

I am an interracial child, mixed with Black and Japanese. I was brought up by my mother due to the divorce of my parents. She never thought of raising me deprived of my nationality or deprived of my dreams, and I admire that. The most positive influence she had on my life is to just teach me to go by my own judgment, and to be straight out honest and to the point. My mother is very impatient, so it *is* best to get right to the point. Our relationship as mother and daughter is real strong, but hey, what do I know, I'm only 14, and we both have a long way to go. The similarities we have are a real weird sense of humor, sensitivity, some habits, and we're both basketball freaks. There probably are more things we have in common, but I just haven't found them yet.

Nikki Mieko Lethridge

*Katsuyo Yamada,
82, housekeeper;
Emiko Ota, 52,
tutor; Leslie
Lethridge, 29,
court clerk, and
her daughter Nikki
Mieko Lethridge,
5, 1977. Katsuyo
Yamada died in
1984.*

Eileen Berger, photographer, with a photograph of her deceased mother, and herself, 1983.

*Audra Hicks
Deckmann, painter,
and Audre
Deckmann Mendel,
53, ballet dancer
and teacher, 1987.*

Lillian P. Nelson, 91,
concert pianist and
singer, and Judith
Nelson Drucker, 54,
impresaria, 1987.

Cidelia Lopez, 82, retired, and Alice L. Comfort, 55, self-employed, 1984.

It is so hard for a mother to stop being a mother when her children grow up. I find myself still trying to protect my daughter who is already a grandmother. When she was very young, it never occurred to me that she could not understand what I demanded of her. Now, when I want something from my grandchild, I know her young mind is only ready to do what she wishes to do. So now I say, "Oh, you are only teasing grandma." That makes her laugh and she knows I understand.

We mothers take things too seriously and our children want to play like puppies. So, if we can play and laugh a little more in the beginning, life could be a little more pleasurable. I know that when my daughter was small, I had to do everything myself, including going to work. This is when the tensions started. Everything had to be done in a hurry. No time to wait for them to dress themselves, to eat by themselves. It was just hurry, hurry. If I had to do it over again, I would want the patience to become completely involved; creating games, and waiting until the child is ready.

I'm amazed at the different views mothers take. Our backgrounds are so different. The attitudes are so different. Some mothers are strict disciplinarians. I changed my attitude with each new children's book that came out. That must have been quite confusing to my daughter. But with all the mistakes, if they were mistakes, we survived. Looking back, I suppose I would do a lot different as a mother with the knowledge I have today, but I realize times have changed and at that time in my young life, I was quite sure that what I was doing for my daughter was right. Maybe I envisioned myself in what I hoped for her at that time. Now I know that the most important quality is her uniqueness in this universe. I am proud to know this person, my daughter. I am delighted she exists and her presence is precious.

Leona Hersh

Mother gave me hope. She read me fairy tales, and she believed in them herself. No matter how difficult life has been—for her and for me—there has been a rock-bottom surety that it would work out in the end. All the dragons would eventually get slain, even if it was painful and scary in the interim.

We are not intimate. My mother is still embarrassed and ashamed of her thoughts and feelings . . . and her facade (and mine) is the barrier. Her heavy feelings (or are they mine?) make me not want to pry because it will feel uncomfortable. Her anxieties and bad self-image are a wedge between us. She's been mad at herself for not being perfect, although she's softer and more accepting of herself now. She hasn't worked out her sexual discomfort.

The most difficult part of our relationship is that she cared too much . . . there was an undercurrent of anxiety and a feeling that she was personally inadequate, which made me feel anxious and also inadequate. I idolized my mother . . . she seemed perfect to me . . . and that made me feel even more inadequate. I was angry that she didn't have higher esteem for herself, and taught me to have a low esteem for myself.

My life has been different from my mother's for many reasons: I was divorced and came out of the structured cocoon; I was able to test my wings and found I could fly. I had therapy and changed the script in my head . . . the one that was so self-critical was changed to a supportive voice. I was able to abate my anxieties, depression, feelings of inadequacy and bad self-image. I also married a man in whose nurturing and loving environment I was able to bloom, and he eventually afforded me financial security.

I'm so pleased that even without therapy my mother has come such a long way toward loving and accepting herself. She is such a beautiful person, and it pleases me that she is beginning to find that out. With all her bad feelings about herself, she has struggled to give us her caring, her wisdom, and even her mistakes. She instilled in me the will to live and achieve. The only thing I would want less of is our constant analyzing because I think this is a way to render the moment powerless. The analysis dissects, and therefore, kills feelings. I would like to let go a little more and just let my feelings flow without fear and my need to control, which keeps me a little distanced from the life and feelings of people who come near me.

As my mother's daughter, I am so happy that I have become my own person, and hear my own voice. I have broken the umbilical cord, and have now come back to my mother as a friend.

Lin Arison

Leona Hersh, 72,
retired, and Lin
Arison, 49, patron
of the arts; 1987.

When I asked my daughter what she wants from her mom, she said, "I just want you to be my mommy, to always be there and love me." After a little thought, she added that she'd like me to take her on lots of trips because she hears our mother always planning trips with us.

The most positive thing that my mother passed on to me that I hope to pass on to my daughter is the love and importance of one's family. To my mother, to me, and I hope to my daughter Jenny, family members are special, and though they may not always meet with your approval, you should overlook everything for the sake of peace and cohesiveness.

One quality that I most admire about my mother is her loyalty. She has had friends for over 50 years. I hope that I, too, have that quality.

My relationship with my mother has not always been smooth. I felt she has often criticized her children needlessly and has not always treated me as a responsible adult.

The biggest change in my relationship with my mother occurred when I was also a mother. I became more tolerant of her and learned to often think of the ways she extended herself to us. I hope that when my daughter is my age she will respect me, think of me as her friend, and want to share her time and thoughts with me as two adults enjoying a positive relationship. My daughter will, I hope, enjoy her life as much as I enjoy being her mother.

Barbara Havenick

Florence Hecht, 70, director of a dog track; Isabelle Amdur, 46, home-maker; and Barbara Havenick, 37, home-maker, with her daughter Jennifer Havenick, 7, 1987.

Adeline Franke, 87;
Bernice Morrison, 69,
retired school nurse;
and Judith Wadsworth,
34, business owner,1982.
Adeline Franke died
in 1987.

*Exie Addison, nearly
100 years old, farmer
and weaver; Isabelle
Yazzie, 61, homemaker
and Navajo nutrition
counselor; Phyllis Ash-
ike, 39, silversmith and
administrative secre-
tary; Lisa Ann Yazzie,
17, student and preg-
nant with her first
child, 1987.*

I was born in 1890, and as far as I know, it was Mississippi. I had four brothers and five sisters . . . I was the oldest, and that's why I got up to 96 years old, oh mercy! One brother and five sisters are still alive, and I have an aunt who's right behind me and she's still alive.

My mother was a good Christian mother, and she trained her girls to be Christian, and how to be houseworkers. I worked on the farm and in the cotton fields; we raised vegetables, chickens, hogs, and cows. In my family, I was like a second little mother . . . taking care of my brothers and sisters, keepin' them from getting hurt, and keepin' their clothes clean . . . I had plenty to do. My father taught the 12th grade in school for 50 years in Mississippi, and when he was absent, Mama took his place in the schoolroom. I went to a local college for Negroes for several years, and taught school myself.

I got married when I was 21 years old, and stopped farming and teaching. I sewed to make my living. I had three children—Beatrice, Katie, and Ophelia. Katie is the second daughter, and all three are still alive. I liked having children of my own, and taking care of them. I liked to train them how to do things. I tried to teach them how to sew and keep house, and how to go to Sunday school. And I trained them that when they went somewhere, how to go and come back, and don't stop and play on the side of the road.

I just took the time as it came. We always had plenty to eat, even though it wasn't what I wanted every time. We had a garden, pecan trees, peanuts, plenty of chickens, and fruit trees. My husband died when my oldest was 14 years old and Katie was eight. We had to get by on our own with little help from others. We would wash and iron clothes for white people . . . we'd boil the clothes in a big pot in the frontyard.

My daughter's been a nurse to me for the past two years ever since I've been sick. She's a nurse and a daughter. I still worry about her when she's out of my sight. She doesn't get home til after dark and I pray every night she comes home safe. Everyday I sit in my room and look at the Virgin Mary, Christ's mother—she seems to get prettier and prettier everyday. There's a sorrow in her heart over the grief of her son.

Abia Stevens

When I was a little girl, my mother loved me and did all she could for me. She taught me the right way to go, and how to love people. She took me to Sunday school, and sent me to school so I could get something in my head and make an honest living. When my mother would send me somewhere to do something for her, she told me not to stop and play, but to come straight home. And that's what I did. I'll always remember that. When a good mother teaches you the right way, you cannot forget it.

I remember Christmas time when she would go downtown to pay Santa Claus to bring me a gift. She would not take me with her because she didn't want me to know. On Christmas Eve night, I would always put my little rocking chair out so Santa Claus could put my gifts in the chair. After he was gone, my mother would wake me . . . I was made so happy. I have a good mother, and I still feel like she's Santa Claus.

My dad passed away when I was eight years old and my mother had three girls. She had to take in washing, and some people paid her very little money. With what she made, she had to pay rent and buy food. When I got old enough to work, I got me a job, and later on I got married. First, I had a baby girl, and then I had two sons. A few years later my husband passed away, so my mother and I had to raise my children. It was hard, but we made it. I wanted to send my daughter to school so she would have a good education. Now, she is on her own and has a good job. We don't act like mother and daughter, we act like sisters. I love her very much, and she says the same about me.

Katie Sims

Abia Stevens, 96, retired school teacher and seamstress, and Katie Sims, 71, housekeeper, 1987.

Here I am, in my 60s with a mother in her 90s, and everything has changed and nothing has changed.

She is still the powerful personality; strong, opinionated, independent, self-sufficient . . . Well, there are times now when she leans on me and I play *mother* to her *child*. I don't always agree with her, but unfailingly, I admire her. She has been a great role model for me. Unusual in the time frame of her age and my age, she has given me the strength to build my own life without fear, but with a great deal of zest, even though our lives and interests have been vastly different.

The hardest part of our relationship has been our common stubbornness. In my earlier years, I often wished my mother had been more of a homebody rather than a career woman. I felt deprived by not having her home when I returned from school. But in my more mature years, I have come to be grateful for that since I don't carry a burden of guilt over a mother's sacrifices, not that she did not make any—but that she lived her life as she needed to, and so freed me to live mine in the same way.

When I was six or seven, in the Vienna of my childhood, my parents often left in the early evening for a night at the opera, the concert, or the theatre. My mother would come into the children's room to kiss us goodnight. As she leaned over me, I would be enveloped by her perfume, her strand of pearls would brush my face, and I would look up at her in admiration, and wonder: Would I ever grow up to be a beautiful, elegant woman like my mother.

Some years ago, my mother, now in her 90s, visited me for a while. I was invited to a party one evening, and before leaving I went to the guest room to wish her goodnight. As I bent over her bed to kiss her, she looked up at me and said, "You look so beautiful, and you smell so good," and I saw my strand of pearls brush her cheek.

Elly Sherman

Erna Oppenheim, 93, retired, and Elly Sherman, 61, artist and poet, 1986.